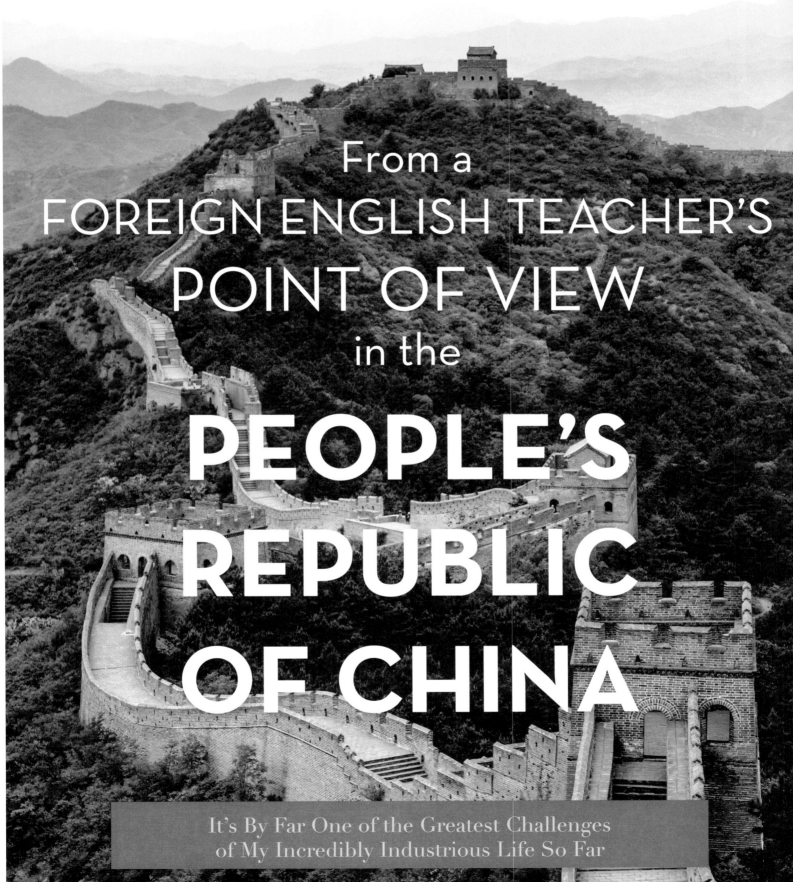

DANNY TELLER

From a
FOREIGN ENGLISH TEACHER'S
POINT OF VIEW
in the

PEOPLE'S REPUBLIC OF CHINA

It's By Far One of the Greatest Challenges
of My Incredibly Industrious Life So Far

ISBN
978-1-5437-4803-1 (sc)
978-1-5437-4804-8 (e)

Print information available on the last page.

To order additional copies of this book, contact
Toll Free 800 101 2657 (Singapore)
Toll Free 1 800 81 7340 (Malaysia)
www.partridgepublishing.com/singapore
orders.singapore@partridgepublishing.com

10/05/2018

PARTRIDGE

Contents

Main Contents

Introduction

Under normal honest circumstances I would really like to make a long list of people, organizations or developments that were responsible for helping or inspiring me to write my spellbinding memoirs

1.) Perhaps the almighty God, should be the first because they enabled me to get the breath of life.

2.) Yvonne Wu, who became my devoted and beloved wife in 2014. She was a much better example compared to my previous marriage in which her continuing encouragement and moral guidance has been invaluable since 2009.

3.) I would also like project empathy and grace to Partridge Singapore Publishers for having patience with me and for making this and other publications, cost effective,

One of the main reasons for my interest in writing is to try to improve the quality life for myself and for as many people in the world as possible. Being recognized by society is a mighty and epic challenge. This is because expecting to receive royalties from an increasingly expectant society simply for the privilege of reading and enjoyment. So, after having written other spellbinding books, I have undertaken a challenge for which I feel is somewhat imperative in the context of residing in my 3rd Non-English speaking country. Not being able to converse properly in Chinese still remains an obstacle. Integrating, in the ever-changing way of life, is as challenging as ever, especially the Orient.

Just for the record: I am a British National who was born in 1964. From 1985 to 2002, I resided in the modern Jewish State of Israel. After leaving this country, I was able to travel and write quite extensively about many additional countries. From my current reckoning in 2018, my tally of lived, visited or business countries is an impressive forty-four. Ever since 1986, I took up a genuine passion in writing large numbers of Travel Biographies, Fiction/Non-Fiction books, Poetry, Fairy Tales, and Songs. Some, have already graced themselves in online format or softcopy including some of my most loyal readers. Others have been written and already waiting for publication: A few others are still subject to be revised and then published. A few books are yet to be written but in the future, this will be rectified.

A breathtaking enterprise began in 2009 when I was fortunate to be able to go on a business trip to the People's Republic of China as an Education Consultant and then change my role to that of a Foreign English Teacher. Yvonne Wu, who is my long-term companion has cared for me ever since that intrepid adventure of a lifetime.

There are other internationally best-selling books from the same author/s.

Five, are all on sale while four more are waiting in queue for publication:

1.) The Eternity of Being a Global Explorer (co-authored by his wife, Yvonne): 2013

2.) Full of Jewish Promise and Spiritual Adventures:2016 (Background of Israelis, The Jewish Religion and the Bible.

3.) The Nepalese Legacy in Short Stories:2016

4.) A first helping of rice, lentils for all to share and care- Part one: 2017

5.) The Challenge of Making Aliyah to (Aretz) The Land of Israel because it was never really a dull moment: Part one: 2018

6.) The Challenge of Making Aliyah to (Aretz) The Land of Israel because it was never really a dull moment: Part two (Yet to be published)

7.) A multitude of Central European Culture in 2013, Subtitled: Absorbing and learning from different points of view. (Yet to be published).

8.) The Malaysian Paradise in all her splendour and glory (Simplicity, peace and serenity) (Yet to be published)

Here is a brief introduction or purpose about the PRC or People's Republic of China. By this I mean in terms of: 1) Popularity; 2) Location; 3) Cost of plane ticket; 4) Cost of basic necessities; 5) Number of tourist attractions which are affordable and expensive; 6) Cost, availability, and reliability of taking methods of public transportation; 7) Hospitality and honesty of the people; 8) Education; 9) Salaries; 10) Realistic and unrealistic expectations of Foreign English Teachers; 11) Languages, communication, and patience; 12) Urban development, infrastructure, and modernization; 13) Blocking websites or censorship. All what is mentioned plus many more reasons than I can think of which prompted me to eventually meet up with Yvonne in the city of Tianjin. For those who have never heard of this place. It's among the five largest cities in China. Its location is about 160km from Beijing in the North East of the country. A high-speed train will take you between the two cities in only thirty-five minutes.

Teaching Treasures from China

Subtitled:
By far one of the greatest challenges of my incredibly industrious life.

This is projected about a nation, people, and land which since 1949, has undergone some radical but necessary changes. Whether those have been good or bad is a never-ending debate. Changes are happening in nearly every part of the world. It depends on how you can react in body and spirit. I normally try to do this systemically and with correct preparation. The very concept of being able to teach Oral or Conversational English as a second language to students has taken a great deal time and effort in the planning. Knowing what and how to teach is matter of practise makes perfect. It's a well-known fact that not every Foreigner who comes to China is able to absorb even the basic Mandarin Chinese. One of the reasons is it's different compared to other languages. Even if you are able to absorb some everyday basic words or phrases, at least you are able to try to understand what is happening around you. There are plenty of bilingual people in China who can translate and make you feel more than comfortable. The first chapter is a devotion mainly to Yvonne Wu. Her invaluable guidance almost from our very first contact online to meeting in person is rapidly approaching 10 years by 2019. That assistance is eternally appreciated.

So, sit back in a comfortable armchair and absorb the never-ending adventures of Danny Teller and Yvonne Wu. They have embarked on an unbelievable new way of sharing life in interchanging and educational frameworks. The demand for ESL Teachers is sought out in many Non-English speaking countries especially in Asia. By and large, this novel is geared to helping you decide whether to come and live in China. If you do forge ahead and take the plunge there are suggestions as to how to find an everlasting and emotional peace plus financial stability.

Yours sincerely

Danny Teller and Yvonne Wu

Chapter 1

The Source: English and Chinese Connection

The book includes literary/morale messages, digital pictures, quality of life issues, different cultures, and adopting different teaching strategies. Of course, there are many more reasons for writing this memoir from time and memorial. If my memory serves me correctly, it was about 5.30 a.m., I was sitting inside my tiny bedsit in the western part of London. For quite some time, I had been an early bird. The date was 9th February 2009. I was preoccupied with my personal laptop. Chatting with people was an ongoing hobby ever since 2004. Eventually I used what at the time were the three most popular chatting online forums, Yahoo Messenger, Skype, and MSN Messenger.

Sending text messages was also trendy in its own right. If you had international SIM card services, regular communication with friends from all over the world was reliable and cheap. If that wasn't sufficient to occupy some of my free time, creative writing in the context of poetry, short stories, song, fairy tales, and even travel biographies only made my daily lifestyle very busy indeed. Since 1986, by far the most profound literary project was dedicated to my pulsating adventures in the Modern State of Israel. This was from the spring of 1984 through to the summer of 2002. In that time, naturally a few travel trips for business and pleasure were made back and forth to England.

Compiling such a monumental story, even in sequels, was hard but not impossible to capture the attention of the media. Still, doing it to use up the time productively, will I hope, remain a hobby for the foreseeable future or if I am fortunate, turn this in into a career. Some of the numerous characteristics which were necessary to achieve this were stubbornness and perseverance. One of the more difficult aspects of undertaking such a project between 2003 to 2009 was having few resources, especially finances. My main occupations in Central and West London were associated with two large successful retail companies, Marks & Spencer and Waitrose. I was in-effect just restocking the shelves with food, giving customer service, and cashier work.

All the coherent daily competencies and obligations were entirely non-managerial but the overall pressure was quite high for a relative salaried employment. Giving good customer service was a key issue, no matter how busy you were or how many other fellow workers were on duty with you at the same time. As one would expect, Bank holidays and weekend attracted more customers because it was outside the nine to five office hours. Even if you were in a non-managerial position, a duty supervisor was on duty at all times of the trading hours to monitor the progress of the staff and deal with necessary customer enquiries.

Working for any retail company, small or large wasn't a part of my plan during my stay in the United Kingdom. I could just remain in the same job until a career change was possible. This could be in the United Kingdom or if I was really fortunate, overseas.

Management, definitely wasn't my plan though that might have helped me get a better salaried position with more pressure. It was even extremely hard to receive an offer for the semi-skilled positions. The main reason wasn't any lack of skill or determination. The number of applications for one position might be over 200. Administrative duties were some of the most difficult jobs to find as I soon found out. It was highly recommended to do the online research beforehand and even then, a lack of practical experience, missing relevant educational documents might be the different between an approval or rejection. I did have an impressive resume so at least my profile wasn't being ignored by the Human Resources Managers. Interviews came my way from time to time but rejection wasn't necessarily due to any fault of mine.

My obligations were basically doing as I was told to do and to the best of my ability with guidance from my peers. Just how many people were in similar positions was hard to know but perhaps they were able to contain their frustrations better than me. As a supermarket assistant, the work shift was divided into the day or evening. The earliest possible start for most of the workers could be as early as 7 a.m. The very latest possible finish was 10 p.m. That depended on what day it was and during a nine-hour shift, 90 minutes were normally allocated for breaks. Because this was in the retail industry, the supermarket was open seven days a week and up to 360 days a year. The only two exceptions for shutting down were Christmas and the New Year.

My life was anything but boring as I was focusing energy on publishing my stories. The opportunity to relocate out of the United Kingdom on a permanent basis was also an eye catcher. If I was really lucky, finding a third and final love of my life was also part of my plan. So, a new career, location, and girlfriend were basic requirements, but was I being over expectant? As fate, would have it, on the morning of the 9th February 2009, something special or rather unusual did happen to me. Whether it was purely random or an act of God, is for your imagination to speculate as a woman contacted me. Yvonne Wu was 39/40 years old and was using an old-fashioned desk top computer at home or at work. That indicated that she was only four and half years my junior. Exactly what prompted her to contact me today will be a mystery or was it out of curiosity. If she was looking for a foreign boyfriend or husband than she had certainly found the right person and commented, "Danny, I am divorced with one son who is at High School. I live in the Wuqing district of Tianjin, which is only just over 30 minutes by high speed train from Beijing. It's a large industrialized city plus an industrialized port with a population of about fourteen million and steadily rising. I work for a foreign trade company with connections to Singapore. Most of my family members are beggars and include, one ageing father, two sisters and one brother. Our lives have been rather sheltered in underdeveloped villages. I have decided to educate myself while the rest of my family remains unaltered. It's hard to foresee any major improvement in the foreseeable future with my other members except for myself."

It was a little difficult to ascertain from the onset of this communication, who was happier and calmer. What did seem evident that both of us would benefit in the short and long term plans. My overall financial situation of living in a developed country wasn't so wonderful but I was much more experienced as a travel writer. Having lived in four countries, had already made me predominately multi-cultural. Yvonne was also in a pressurized situation but, unlike me she was not suffering from outstanding or cohering debts. The home she was living in with her son belonged to her but it was defined as being in poverty. Though the government was planning on some project renewal, the exact date for this happening was another two to three years from now.

We were connected by something called "trying to do something about it." This was the hope and belief which projected on a better style of living. By and large, people complained far too much about the challenges of life. But all too often, little or nothing was being done to rectify the situation. I respected those from the very bottom of my heart those that were prepared to make an effort.

Yvonne and I were self-educated in a manner of speaking but our cultural and social backgrounds were so very different. That was because we grew up in contrasting parts of the world. An eight-hour time difference separated us but that didn't really matter because of IT or information technology. Sure, enough there were a few long conversations in simultaneous periods but not necessarily at the same time. The length of each chat depended on how much free time and of course how convenient it was to communicate.

So, now that we had confirmed this friendship, now it was time to discuss the possibility of meeting up in person for the first time. Going all the way to China definitely wasn't a part of my plan for a few years. But most plans didn't always go according to how you wanted. If I did go to Beijing on holiday it would be only after my annual bonus was paid in March of 2010. And just two weeks would be allocated at the very most. Longer periods were permitted from my bosses at Waitrose but a special request needed to be applied for well in advance so a replacement could be found during my absence. A standard tourist visa was required to visit China but using a British Passport, this was very easy to get an approval. If Chinese nationals wished to visit the United Kingdom the process as expected was much more complicated. Following the next few sets of conversations Yvonne popped up an unexpected suggestion which was really out of the blue. She thought I might seriously consider coming as a teacher and not just for a vacation. These types of jobs were classified as ESL or English as a second language.

My real dream, prior to this suggestion was being an editor, journalist or even foreign correspondent. My extensive travel experience was one of the reasons why, plus my journals. Alas, with no sound background in this career under my belt so it was still relegated to being a hobby. Being paid for doing something that you truly loved was a privilege. The world of editing was not just very competitive but risky. This was due to libel or derogative comments emphasized on people and organizations without notarized agreements. This is turn could trigger off a genuine risk of litigation. The media could tell the society some truths about sensitive issues but the high-risk factors often resulted in journalists ending up in prison or even tragic loss of life. This was a result of people meddling around with the affairs of total strangers especially in the more underdeveloped regions of the world.

However, many wonderful adventures were still in the making. That depended on the coherent situation, writer, people, and underlying circumstances. To me, it was still worth my while to try and tell the world about what happened and why. My adventures leading up to 2018 have taken me to as many as 44 countries. The foundation of some of my work relates to the, how, why, when, and purpose. During my stay in the United Kingdom, it was a nice thought to have been able to undertake some more volunteering positions as I had done in Nepal. My previous experiences in one of the poorest parts of the world appealed to me very much. The job situation was so hard that leaving any employment and having to find another one upon my return was no longer so realistic. So, with the pros and cons of being a foreign correspondent or volunteering it was hard to know exactly what phase of action to try next? Yvonne then pointed out that there was no point in staying in a supermarket any longer. It was as she defined as nothing less than a dead-end job. There was still a need to support myself but from a Chinese point of view my accent, nationality, mother language, and white skin were advantageous. She also mentioned that before it was too late, the prospects of working and living in China were still good. If I came over, the Ministry of Foreign Affairs would recognize me as being a Foreign Expert. Of course some details relating to my educational background was important but depending on how qualified you were it was virtually possible for native English speakers to walk straight into a job with only some basic questions asked.

If the schools thought that you could perform the job right away the invitation or job offer would be offered to you. The salaries and conditions of work depended on a number of additional factors which included; gender, age, preferred city, type of visa you would enter China, expected duration, free or rental assisted accommodation, number of classes/office hours, assessments on your overall performance and strategies, overtime or extra curriculum activities, bonuses or extra entitlements, and probatory period. The issue of relocation from one country to another for whatever reasons, seemed to be quite a nice idea. Living in Israel, America, and Nepal had prepared me to be more mature and flexible. Living in China was supposed to be quite a challenge. Understanding some Chinese was a basic advantage but I didn't even know one single word. During my chatting and some corresponding emails Yvonne showed me some translations for my stories but I wasn't able to read any of the script. That, really was the least of my concerns for the moment. My manager at Waitrose was informed of my intentions to go to China. There was a benefit which was given to all employees of up to 90 days' unpaid leave. In that time, I had to try and sort out my affairs in China and then resign by email. More or less at the same time, I received an invitation letter from a special agency for a F1 Visa which permitted me to visit China for up to 90 days. Depending on the type of plane ticket I bought, an extension of up to one year was allowed. However, the initial travel ticket had to show just 90 days so the airport authorities would authorize my initial entry into the country. There was a charge of just sixty-four pounds at the Chinese Embassy for the service. The number of airlines was quite extensive which offered prices from London Heathrow to Beijing. In the end, Emirates who were based in Dubai had the best value at 450 English Pounds. For cancelling and rescheduling, an extra 50 pounds was charged. The 90-day F visa application was processed and approved in just three working days. Yvonne had been able to send me the equivalent of about 400 English pounds to my bank account to help me buy the round ticket. Just how she was able to save up the money since February I will never know. I needed a supplementary 50 pounds to pay the balance and so towards the end of August of 2009, I was more or less ready for what could and should be one of the biggest alterations in my life since 1985.

At that period, I had emigrated to Israel but the circumstances were a little different because of Law of Return for all Jews since 1948. In 2002, my 90-day stay in America was given to all British passport holders. Being in Nepal as a coordinator for nearly six months from 2002/2003, was easy because of tourist visa extensions which were normally needed every 30 days. So having a British passport did have its advantages. To be quite frank, leaving my tiny bedsit in West London and going to Heathrow Airport felt a little funny. Would my friendship with Yvonne be stable enough to be able to settle down in the Far East? Just to make matters a little more difficult, Yvonne confirmed that being made redundant from the very beginning of September, wasn't her fault. We would in effect be together during an initial period of relative mental, morale, and financial instability. Though I had been in much worse situations, those problems were solved and dealt with appropriately. Compared to how I lived in England, Israel, America, and Nepal I wasn't prepared to believe that China would be any more difficult. It was also time for me and Yvonne to focus on developing everlasting values of love, admiration and eternal bondship, from time and memorial.

Chapter 2

Many cities such as Tianjin, Beijing, Shanghai, Guangzhou

This chapter will be quite a short one and devoted to provinces, cities and sizeable towns in China. For a relatively long period of time in history, China has been one of the largest countries in the world. It also has housed by far the world largest population which was estimated to be between 1.3 to 1.5 billion inhabitants. There were thirty-four provinces in total with some being larger than other. That depended which part of the country as well as how well it was developed. Apart from Hong Kong, Tianjin, Beijing, Shanghai and Tibet, I wasn't so familiar with other places in China. Because, Kong Kong was classified as being out of the mainland, all Chinese nationals needed permission to visit there.

Some of the largest cities in China were called Guangzhou and Shenzhen with populations of between 10 to 20 million or more. Beijing and Shanghai were still the largest cities with a minimum of 20 million and getting bigger. The reason for the expansion was due to rapid urbanization which in effect would try to eradicate poverty at some point in the future. Wuxi, Wuhan, Jinan, Suzhou, Hangzhou and Zhengzhou, all had populations of between 5 to 10 million as well as competing for international trade and tourism. So, if this was your first time it was a little hard to know which city or place to choose from until you were able to do some exploration in person. If you applied for a position from outside of China, then the company were supposed to pick you up from the nearest airport. Most of the main cities had an airport, train bus station for transportation purposes. If no airport was available due to lack of urban development, one would eventually be in the planning stage unless that was not environmentally or economically recommended. Picking and choosing any position from inside China was much easier because you were already orientated with part of the geography and mentality. Yvonne found me a company straight away in 2009. One of the issues was the accuracy, interpretations and honesty of the information from the website. Most of the websites were in Chinese unless English was available. If the information was inconclusive, it was basically guessing and trying to figure out the meaning. Meeting up with the representatives in whichever city was also a matter of finding out at the very last moment. The size and infrastructure of the city determined the salaries and quality of life. The cheaper the city, the school or agency would rent out a flat for you or give you a dormitory. Investment was a big issue because no-one wanted to lose money. If the cost of living was considered to be too expensive only a rental subsidy was offered for an apartment with the rest of the costs being entirely at your expense. Whatever agreement was signed, negotiating also depended on experience and qualifications. Teachers with less experience would receive lower salaries which would give more than enough time and space for them to learn the best methods before the contract expired. Then there was something defined as being high risk areas or larger cities. Most of this densely populated and well developed. Many security and legality checks occurred to make sure everything was in order. Being safer and more isolated in the countryside was another option because the police would generally leave you alone. No matter wherever you went to work, China was undergoing rapid and stringent changes which would affect you sooner, rather than later. A contract was also in consideration for changes especially before renewal. Some of the schools were located in isolated places or well off the beaten track. Others were within easy access including public transportation and shopping mall. Life was more than abundant all over China with all provinces having one provisional or capital city of at-least one million residents. There were many other small towns and villages dotted almost everywhere.

But let's imagine that for arguments sake, that you have just stepped off the plane at Beijing city airport. Once you have cleared through immigration and baggage check, representatives from the school or agency who hired you will have picked you up and will do their utmost to help you settle down. That includes familiarizing yourself with the school campus and a place to live. China is not your country of origin so the language barrier will be one of your main problems as well as the feeling of alienation. Other foreigners go through the same process upon first arrival in the country. But don't rely on any foreigners to provide comfort or a shoulder to rest on. If you are lucky, a few might offer some guidance but most will say they have no patience and leave you alone. That sounds a little daunting but don't worry. Get on with the job of acclimatization and absorption which is the main focus on my next chapter. I often tend to try and figure out what to do in new places all by myself, rather depend on others to do it for me. When this is done, I will find the route to happiness is much easier. What I have attempted to do to the best of my ability is to make sure that your initial visit as a foreign teacher will go as smoothly as possible. I came to China in September 2009 and now it's already the autumn and winter of 2018. More than nine years have elapsed in which by far the most pressurized period was the first two to three years. I was resolute to finding a solution which worked for me and in the process, I tried to create a new way of life on a permanent basis in the country. It can be done because if I can try my utmost to help myself, then so can you. Once you have fathomed out the system to a lesser or greater extent, the rest is yours for the asking.

Chapter 3

Realization of being in a professional teaching capacity

Physical and emotional reality is always rather arduous to describe as to being in a new place. Chatting online with Yvonne and the agency who invited me to come was only one moral aspect. The sense of orientation is a good method of getting on with the job in hand and not worrying about the unknown. My next realization was that China is my 3rd Non-English speaking country. That indicated a little less patience to absorb a new dialect compared to when I was much younger. In as much as foreign languages are still very much a love of my life, I now consider them to be of less importance. This wasn't necessarily due to tardiness or a lack of care. I also began to wonder how much more information is needed to absorb to find unconditional peace. I have no answer to this question because my main passion was to find a strong position in the world of journalism. Until that dream occurs, my teaching job is of no less importance.

The realization of not knowing even one single word in Mandarin Chinese in 2009 proved to be a big issue in navigation, acclimatizing, communication, and eating the local food. Getting used to the way of life like the Chinese would eventually be second nature. I knew that it was a matter of time before that happened but I had to focus on the fact that I had no writing job. Some of my adventures might be a focus for informative lessons including exploration. Yvonne reminded me a great number of times that my accent, nationality and color of skin was sought after by so many schools. The next fundamental realization was purely and solely on teaching conversational English rather than grammar. Conversational English was also defined as being only oral or the ability to pronounce the language properly. Chinese teachers had obligations for focusing on grammar but with poor speaking. A foreign teacher's main competencies unless written on the contract are to make the students speak. If grammar was requested the benefits, obligations, pressure, and assessments increased. Teaching grammar came in different formats because it was very complex.

1.) IELTS: International English Language Testing System.

2.) TOEFL: Test of English as a Foreign Language.

3.) TEFL: Teaching English as a Foreign Language.

4.) SAT: Scholastic Assessment Task.

5.) ACT: American College Test.

6.) GRE: Graduate Record Examinations.

7.) GMAT: Graduate Management Admission Test.

8.) PTE: Pearson Test of English.

9.) CELTA: Certificate in English Language Teaching to Adults.

Those were some examples which varied according to difficulty. Many foreigners including myself concluded that life was made much easier with oral English. Salaries and other benefits were lower but your monthly or yearly income was still considered to be above average compared to most Chinese nationals. Not only that but at least you will not suffer from insomnia. Naturally, I had a few doubts as to my teaching ability. Nervousness and lack of confidence did prove to be hard to overcome at first. Behaving in a mature fashion needed to be part of my system. The strategies in the classrooms or office would eventually be modified to suit my personal needs. No two lessons were identical even if the material was repeated about 10 times. Some of my confidence, stability, and perseverance could be improved by observing other teachers. Of course, a great deal of trial and effort would be activated but knowing exactly how to teach was a specialized skill. That will be my main focus in the next two chapters but I didn't meet any foreigner who was a genius overnight. Oral English was a lot of fun and Chinese students would be receptive if you put effort to find the best way. Another way of putting it was that I had already left my home in the United Kingdom. I had taken unpaid leave from my boss. My financial situation was still defined as being unstable but the main compensation was having all the freedom in the world since 2002 to do as I so wished. Being happy and content with what I had decided to do in China was still a hard question to answer. Speaking subjectively, the facilities including IT skills would enable me to perform in and out of work. Not only that, but it was necessary to avoid any projection of negative comments which circulated behind my back. Perhaps some foreigners expected far too much from the Chinese. Or could it be that the Chinese were over expectant from foreigners. The levels of students ranged from Pre-school to University or even Adults. If you chose or preferred to do the lower levels, much less pressure was focused on your overall performance. Higher levels of students would drastically affect the methods and attitudes. As a matter of fact, ESL salaries were higher for small kiddies so long as the teachers had enough and relevant patience and strategies. Just how this was done was your business and coordinating with your assistants. To the best of your abilities, try to verify the obligations, rewards or punishments for your daily, weekly or monthly performances. If coming to China seems too daunting a challenge, the same procedure is no doubt similar in other Non-English speaking countries. Whatever you decide to do to help make up your mind, this chapter has given some insight with some invaluable advice. At least give it a shot before giving up before the going gets too tough. But if you find that teaching in any grammatical or oral capacity really isn't for you than all I can do is wish you a Bon Voyage and Bonne Chance for a new career elsewhere.

Chapter 4

Teaching strategies/methods/facilities Part one

You must remember that I was like many other teachers who came to China with very little knowledge of conducting affective and professional teaching methods. My Nepalese program was in a different environment and circumstances. From a foreign English teacher's point of view, I have been able to stay much longer than expected. In terms of advice, the information which is provided will emphasis on positive innovation or methods. If that is exactly what you are looking for, I will be delighted to try to point you in the right direction to the best of my ability. But I must warn you that whatever method you try, might not be easy at the beginning. Practise does make perfect and regardless of how talented you think that you are, no school in China taught me how to be a teacher. I was assessed from time to time no matter how experienced I was. It didn't matter what level the students were or if they wanted to learn. Sometimes I got it right and sometimes I got it wrong. Almost all what I have had to learn since my arrival was done predominately alone. Occasionally I had teaching assistants and other foreign English teachers to offer advice but not much else. No-one did my lesson for me so I could observe and do next to nothing.

Teaching strategies/methods/facilities, *are by and large, entirely up to the foreign teacher, the assistants and the school leaders. It may vary from place to place but the infrastructure is generic.*

My educational back ground prior to 2009 stemmed from England, Israel, and Nepal. England was my country of birth. I learnt the modern Hebrew language plus some IT skills. A primitive school in Nepal provided me the first real framework as educational coordinator for a few months. Some of those wonderful adventures have been turned into stories and are available in:

1.) Full of Jewish Promise and Spiritual Adventures: (Background of Israelis, The Jewish Religion and the Bible: 2016

2.) The Nepalese Legacy in Short Stories:2016

3.) A first helping of rice, lentils for all to share and care- Part one:2017

My adventures in Nepal have been compared to accomplishing a total miracle out of virtually nothing in a small and remote village. Absorption into the village was very easy which enabled me to absorb about 800 to 1000 standard Nepalese words and phrases. During my two-year military service in the (IDF), Israeli Defence Forces my Hebrew was fluent enough to communicate with other soldiers and my commanders.

Stepping into classrooms was by far one of the greatest challenges of my life so far. These activities were varied according to what happened, but let's imagine for arguments sake that that most of the foreigners coming to China or those who are already teaching, can't speak or understand the language properly enough. It's not the easiest of languages to absorb but even those foreigners that can form a basic dialogue, there will almost always be local teachers to help you get orientated with the local policies and customs. Just one of them is what I describe as being Dress Code. I might otherwise define these as what clothes you wish to wear anywhere in a school.

Dressing properly in any public area is a mental strategy to approaching this job. If you want to be formal or informal, at least be clean and tidy. This is especially true for when the students see you for the very first time. You will always be noticed in many areas of the school campus. If you decide to be more formal, wear a long or short sleeved shirt. That also depends on the climate. The colors or patterns doesn't really matter but I recommend plain white or as few patterns as possible. White shirts are also much more professional. The trousers can be black, blue, dark brown, dark green but not too bright or shiny. A tie is often optional unless the school is absolutely adamant that one should be worn at all times. During the hot summer months, heat stress is much stronger and so ties are normally exempt. Shoes need to be black or dark brown and preferably, fully cover your feet. Sandals, unless this is a summer job, are to be avoided at any times. I have seen foreigners wearing open sandals and shorts in the summer time during full time jobs. If possible, don't create too much attention to yourself by what you wear other what is really or absolutely necessary. Everyone, at the school including other foreigners define you as an expert for providing invaluable information. Standing in front of the students and local teachers indicates that you are also being used for marketing and promoting their educational services.

My first interactions with schools and students was a tendency to have negative or misleading projections. My dress code was inappropriate for the first two or three years so some major changes were implemented to make me look a little more decent. Rest assured, that some foreigners appear to be so untidy and this made me look rather smart in comparison. Though each school is different, the wearing of jeans, t-shirts and training shoes is not advisable. One of the reasons are visible gaping holes and loose strands around the knees. This, from most points of view might just look a little weird. Even in the less well salaried jobs, there is more than adequate funding to purchase suitable clothing in a variety of styles. A beggar like approach might not give a good impression in the school and a reluctance for the headmaster to renew your contract. If training shoes are to be worn, at least compliment them with a matching sports outfit.

Female foreign teachers are a little luckier because they can wear a combination of trousers, skirts, dresses or even formal dress suits. Putting on make-up or jewellery is not advisable though some simple types of earrings are fashionable and attractive. The men should be cleanly shaved at all times and those with beards and moustaches should be trimmed once a week. A haircut every four to six weeks won't break your bank account either. If females have longish hair, tie it like a pony tail with a colorful ribbon/band if necessary but those with short hair, make sure it's nice and neat. If you really wish to change your dress code to something much more casual, doing it during social gatherings and sports meetings is highly preferable.

And now to the sensitive subject of Obesity. I don't wish to sound too rude or immodest to anyone but there is an awful lot of unnecessary and self-inflicted obesity in the world. Being overweight or grossly overweight is a direct cause of: bad/irregular eating habits, gross lack of exercise which causes suffering from one or more seemingly incurable illnesses.

I have noticed a large number of obese people including Chinese and foreigners. Perhaps, from a purely multicultural prospective, males in most countries including China are fatter than the females. Males are proportionately lazier than females but an incredible quantity of junk food is eaten by both sexes nearly every day. Even at the elementary schools, boys and girls are walking around with big or flabby stomachs, but the boys are out-quantifying the girls. Protruding stomachs with foreigners in a classroom doesn't look so wonderful in front of students. If you have an acute medical problem, try to shed that fat from your stomach with regular balanced meals. There are more than plenty of doctors who will give you an examination at the local hospital which won't cost you an arm or leg. Try some form of physical or domestic routine such as shopping, cleaning, walking in the park. It might be a nice change to sitting for hours on end playing with your mobile and laptop. In every country, cultural holidays, weddings, birthdays, graduations or new jobs will affect your working and social life. Calorie rich foods might be offered to you but if you really must refuse than do it so as not offend anyone in the process. I was invited for a number of celebrations mostly in my first year. A lot of unnecessary excessive weight was put on due to lack of exercise. Teaching can also cause extensive hours in front of the computer preparing material or chatting. There is more than enough free time even if you are not enthusiastic in sports to buy a push bicycle which is available from the many varieties, and at affordable prices.

Having a sound mental attitude is one of the most important attributes with teaching. It's not my fantasy job from a professional point of view but as an alternative, this is just as acceptable and rewarding. What a privilege to be able to walk into a classroom with some 30 to 40 students and sometimes local teachers looking at me. Naturally there are those who are shy or nervous. Occasionally the students are fidgety, some are curious, but some are eager to learn while others indicate no interest at all in learning anything. I always take the liberty to prepare my materials well in advance plus writing some key words or phrases on the backboard or whiteboard. Some foreigners might very well come to China because they conclude that living better is a unique opportunity to grasp. It's possible that some might come for a drastic change in scenery, salary, and general conditions of work. For heaven's sake, don't come because you have absolutely no choice. Genuine happiness will not be found if that is your real reason. Your attitude needs to absorb the new environment in which people have accepted you into their lives. Some foreigners might even prefer to use this job as a stepping stone to go on to something even better. Starting up a language or training center is just one example but make sure your focus is on your job and have realistic expectations. Rest assured, that the quantity of backchat which circulates from local teachers to students is perfectly normal. Though your level of Chinese is not good enough to understand every word, at least have some idea of what is going on. Behave normally at all times during lessons because not everything goes according to split second timing. One example might be that an active lesson might be followed by a noisy one and you are not to blame for this. Modifications are necessary but chose your methods very carefully on how to execute this even if it's at the spur of a moment. I often claim that if you have a right attitude and do the job from the bottom of your heart than people will notice it. Your mental attitude needs to be as flexible and mature as possible even at the expense of absorbing some constructive criticism.

I often feel that a number of foreign teachers in China are coming from their countries of origin with the aim of doing whatever they wish is acceptable. That is not exactly true but acclimatization is a normal procedure related to expectations and the local mentality. Luckily, for foreigners, there is no-one standing over you with a whip as if you are a slave. Whatever you do, honor the rules and regulations of the school and try to become a part of the furniture. Even with all my international exploration, settling down took me quite a bit longer than I expected.

Alas I have unfortunately met a number of highly academically qualified teachers who came with forceful or immodest attitudes. Some of the very worst examples are those from the much more developed Western regions of the world especially America. The men are the very worst examples compared to the woman. Typical behavior can be indicated by: Showing off; being snobs; indicating extreme levels of arrogance; thinking that they are the best teachers in the world; forcing their ideas on other foreigners and believing that their strategic methods are far superior. Without giving any personal names or explicit details about what happened, it's important to realize that that showing off makes everyone around you feel uncomfortable. Naturally, no further contact remains with those people or organizations but those incidents still remain distant memories.

In some circumstances, institutions only have need for only one foreigner. If their needs are greater, than two are required. If more than five foreigners are teaching in the same school or institution, try to honor their duty and presence. A proportionate amount of Middle and High schools are associated with sending students overseas to continue their studies. A quantity of specialized foreigners is needed for academic topics to greatly enhance the ability of the students. The subjects range from whatever is needed to be achieved. I have been in at least one school in the Wuqing district of Tianjin where a large number of foreigners were divided up into High/Middle or Primary departments. Some of more advanced teachers were on much higher salaries but the pressure they were under was considerably more. I would highly recommend you to stand firm and be happy with your teaching job whatever you are doing. Being the only foreigner in one school from my prospective has considerable amounts of advantages. There might also be, clashes of personalities, ideas, and strategies. And don't forget that your concept of teaching might be totally different to someone else.

Immodesty between foreigners will cause also cause tension and might not allow those who are more humble and modest to do their jobs well. Respect the foreigners if the school or agency asks you to share the same apartment with another. Try to respect the foreigners in the same office or the very next office. Sometimes a foreigner might be teaching with a load voice which can be a little off-putting. Remember, you can't be friendly with everyone and any time you so wish. If you feel friction causing tension, the best action is to try to avoid all communication until the situation calms itself down. On the other hand, you will occasionally bump into teachers who are prepared to pool their resources together. Some might even give you useful material to see what they are doing. Accept this gracefully and give them something back in return. Swapping files between foreigners became a regular habit of mine mainly since 2011. Even now, several years later this trend has steadily continued. My personal encyclopedia has grown so incredibly massive that I have actually forgotten the exact number of files I have accumulated. This is something for which I am extremely proud of. You can be sure that just about every topic and level are catered for with maturity and knowledge. Increased IT skills and time management help me to stay well on top and in control. Being modest in China means respecting all the laws and regulations. Speaking from my personal prospective I am humble at all times in what and how I try to teach. I have never once dared to show off about how good I think I am or was. One day might be inactive while the next will be much more lively. Be modest to the student's feelings and remember one very important factor. This is their country and education especially during their youth or adolescence. You were invited to come and teach, so do the job as instructed with some relevant changes to the best of your ability. Even if you are reprimanded from time to time, absorb the information and use your diligence to make amends. I am certain that no-one can perform with 100% accuracy every single lesson. If that were the case that person would classified as a genius. My personal goal is to achieve a minimum success of 50% and a maximum of 75%. That is a modest and realistic goal. If I drop below 50 there is a need to modify and occasionally I can achieve more than 75%. That indicates that all the hard mental and physical preparation, paid dividends.

Since 2009, modesty made me take a very different attitude about trying to make China my permanent home. It was a realistic approach for which confronted me when it was least expected. I was under the distinct conclusion that this career might be the only realistic one which was achievable before I got too old. By the year, 2019 I will already have achieved fifty-five years old. That is still young enough to establish a long-lasting career while a large number of people in the world go through life with little or no hope of any profession. A gross lack of finances, resources, poor geographical location, lack of time, patience, desire, and no hope are some of the many reasons why this is so often a reality.

Strategies in the classroom

In order to be able to begin to define about how I would teach in the classroom it's necessary to learn suitable methods referring to: Mental attitudes of foreign teachers and students: Patience and Time Management. The allocated time per class can be anything from 40 minutes, to as much as two hours. That depends on the levels and number of students.

The IT facilities, the amount of light in the classroom or office, curriculum, level of noises, energy, ventilation, eating, and hygiene, will determine how a teaching job can be performed. Of-course the facilities' and general conditions of work are different from school to school. From my perspective, a great deal of time, desire, energy, and some heard earned money was needed to adopt a suitable strategy.

At least three years or more were needed which was an acceptable time for additional refinement. Mental preparation was one of the most crucial learning strategies even before you physically step into a classroom. You mind needs time management which can also defined as split second timing. Of course not everything goes according to clock work. Sometimes, backup material is needed even at the last moment. The school has given you a text book or text books which are being used by the local bilingual teachers. No-one is telling exactly how to teach but some guidelines can often be used and books are merely pieces of information. Depending on how fussy the headmaster is, you need to be more exact in what and how you wish to teach. Change the lesson plan according to what you are convinced is educationally interesting and factual. If you need to deviate don't overdo it to avoid being reprimanded. Smiling with your students from time to time is necessary to make everyone feel more comfortable. You might find out that all they want from you is to have some fun and games. As long as they can learn something, full steam ahead and boy voyage.

In most schools throughout China, there are modern or up-to-date IT facilities in the classrooms. This includes a computer, projector and speakers. Those classrooms that are still old fashioned, they will eventually make way for advanced systems. All you need to do is after turning it on is plugging in your memory stick or external hard drive. Then you can open as many files as you wish to use. Viruses are one of the biggest problems because many people use exactly the same system. Most schools still use Windows 7 which are prone to getting viruses and perform very slowly. Apple computers, which are more reliable and expensive but they don't get affected by viruses. It's very rare for an Apple computer to break down. If Microsoft is being used than anti-viruses can be used from time to time to clean up the infections. Have a back-up of a memory stick or external hard drive in case this happens. Memory sticks, micro cards can store smaller amounts of data compared to external hard drives. Most foreigners now use at least four Terabytes (TB) though smaller or larger quantities are available online if necessary. One Terabyte (TB) equals 1000 Gigabytes. Now that might very well sound an awful lot but as we accumulate incredible quantities of data on a yearly basis, the space is quickly used up:

In the very unlikely scenario that the school is not able to provide computerized equipment, it's back to the drawing board with a blackboard or whiteboard. 99% of all foreigners that I met since coming to China use desktops or laptops. Those teachers who are doing it the old-fashioned way, soon find out it's not so practical.

Most foreigner's own a laptop, iPhone, an iPad or even an E-reader. Some own even two laptops. This is because the higher salaries enable them to buy the equipment. Schools should provide at least one reliable all in one printer, scanner, and photocopier. If it's color be grateful but black and white is almost always available. If no computers are set up in the classroom a projector is available with a special lead which can connect directly to your laptop. Due to rapid modernization, let's take it step further in the right direction with electronic screens and loud speakers. This is simplicity and reliability but using the Windows 7 software is not so reliable and prone to viruses. I have used electronic screens in a few schools now and it's amazing how straightforward this system is. There is also a USB port to plug in your memory stick or external hard drive. All that is needed is to tap on the files and open them up.

Some 40 years ago, I would never have believed in my wildest dreams that such modernized IT systems would be a new way of life. Note books and text books might even one day find their way into museums. Whatever other gadgets are in the making, this enables nearly all tasks possible at the touch of some buttons. Even from as early as grade one primary level, students are already IT proficient with most gadgets especially mobile phones. Using them in the classroom is not normally allowed except for teachers because it's a part of their work.

When teaching in a classroom, the general facilities are only one aspect of your work. Smiling and being cheerful is just as crucial. Having confidence is another but you must know exactly what you are going to teach during each and every lesson. Even if the school gives you a general curriculum in the form of a text book use it but change if and when necessary. There might even be some extra special modules which you need to make. I don't believe that I have met one single foreigner in China who goes exactly according to the text book. Even if the text book appears to be misleading, allow the Chinese teachers to use it according to how they want to. Do what you want to but respect peoples' wishes in the interests of the students and no-one will have cause to bring up a complaint. Strategies can be determined with many other factors such as: The time of the day, week, month or even year. There might be many or a few students in the classroom. Be careful with what topic you choose plus levels of distractions. If you are tired take it easy especially if the noise levels are higher than normal. Maybe you are accompanied with a TA (teaching assistant) or local teacher? Are you feeling nervous or confident? Most classes in full time jobs are 40 or 45 minutes. Are the students doing homework during the 10-minute break? Are there any absentees? Are the students in a good mood to learn? Sometimes they can't be bothered to do anything at all. Try to go along with their desire so have some fun so long as you can control them.

Greet them with a hi, hello, good morning, good afternoon or even good evening. A good-evening only comes up in make-up classes or some cultural activities. Make up classes might crop up at the weekends but very rarely on Saturdays and Sundays. If, in the event that it does, it normally occurs just before or after public or national holidays. They are listed as follow:

1.) The Chinese New Year – January or February.

2.) The Sweeping Tomb – Normally April.

3.) May Day – Always May.

4.) Dragon Boat Festival- Always June.

5.) Teacher's Day- Normally September.

6.) Mid-Autumn Festival – Normally September.

7.) National Holiday- Always October.

8.) New Year – Always January1st.

9.) Christmas Day is optional in which you are obligated to work if the school requires it.

Of course, there are other holidays such as Mother's Day, the Magic Lantern Festival, Army Day. Whether the school decides to have a rest is up to the discretion of the head master. A public school normally operates five days a week. Monday to Friday. Training Centers operate from Tuesdays to Sundays, with Mondays and Tuesdays off. There is a very big difference between the two which I will explain a little more later on.

Let's imagine that if the classroom is quiet when you walk in so after a brief greetings message, then explain what you are going to teach today. There might very well be a review from the previous lesson or a song to listen to. Try a game which is also an ice-breaker. It's hard to know exactly what the students prefer because they might be of different opinions. One of the biggest barriers, is getting the students to speak one to five word sentences at a time. Most sentences will be one to three words at the very most. Those who can perform between 5 to 10 words with or without mistakes need a great deal of practice and patience. You might wish to teach about their favorite sport, in or out of school. Another good topic is a potential career for 5 to 10 years' time.

The time management methods vary from lesson to lesson and levels of mental exhaustion. Repeating yourself over and over again is boring so alternate the way in which you do it. Even if this is at the spur of a moment it doesn't really matter but make it practical and humorous. Try to joke along with the nosiest of students but exercise a degree of strictness. Whatever you do, don't be a monster and you are not allowed to verbally or physically abuse anyone. Take a keen interest in what they are doing and that will help you to blend into the environment as well as raising your morality.

Indicate to them that you mean business but you are happy to be with them. Please don't waste too much useless energy even if the students will not keep quiet. Stand there for a few moments until all is calm and then continue. Losing your voice or developing laryngitis is a teacher's nightmare. It happened to me a few occasions or about once every two years. Being ill is not really recommended and taking medicine is an absolute must until your health returns to normal. If the lesson is fast and active, keep up the good work. Students speaking individually or in pairs are just two methods. Working in larger groups can also be done. If there is a quiz, try to divide them into two. Some teaching methods are based on technical information which is all very fine. If you compare this to the more creative/artistic side, there is a very big difference. Focusing on educational games is a fun way to teach. This is also known as PPTs or PowerPoints which are extremely popular. In 2009, I never used this method because I didn't know how it worked. Eventually I came across local and foreign teachers who used them quite a lot. Not long afterwards did I realize how effective it was. By 2011, I had only a handful of PowerPoints and a very large number of Word Documents. Excel was used more commonly for math's, grading or statistics. So, I decided to turn or convert most of my files to PowerPoints. It was interesting to see just how many varieties that were possible. Upon completion, each file needed to be categorized, numbered into what are known as folders. The more information I received or made, the larger number of extra folders were needed. Eventually, I managed to develop a huge encyclopedia and this is still in constant need of refinement. The organization is so accurate that I more or less know where a file is located according to the topic. From time to time I will forget so I have a unique management system which helps me to track what I need to use.

Being a teacher in a classroom is now more or less second nature. My mental system has made me believe that this is where I am supposed to be at this period of my life. As time progressed, my potential for being over average was soon realized. The Time Management issue also needed to be as precise as possible but knowing how long to spend on each segment was not so easy. If students did well I was able to get most or all of them to speak at least once in the classroom. Those who had trouble to understand, then more translation was needed or in some cases rephrasing.

A PowerPoint contains relevant information in which the material can be reviewed depending on the overall capabilities of the students. It was a lot of trial and error with more than one file open if necessary. Games can be used from time to time as long as it develops a humorous and beneficial atmosphere to the students. If an idea came into my mind I wrote it down on a piece of paper or typed up some words or sentences as a reminder of what this material would or might be. The main preparation would continue at home or in the classroom. After a total of only four years in China; 2009 to 2013, it felt as if I was heading in the right direction as I focus on more methods and concepts in the next chapter.

Chapter 5

Teaching strategies/methods/facilities Part two

From 2013 to 2018, I found myself in a somewhat coveted position of being defined as a true Professional Foreign Teacher. Whatever strategies I had used or experimented did, seem to work. If changes were needed they were only minor ones but I like to imagine that: Every class was a new mental and physical challenge. Each and every class I was standing up or sitting down and contributing to the educational competencies of the students. Each class I was also benefitting from my endeavours and loyalty. It was necessary to greet the students as well as saying farewell. I even managed to absorb some basic conversational Chinese but it was not really good enough to be understood in society. Power cuts did happen from time to time but that didn't affect me too much. I eventually came to a unanimous conclusion to buy a portable speaker and projector in case the system at school was not up to standards. If this was classified as relying too much on IT well the same could be said about most teachers in China. Nothing is infaluable so we need to deal with all the relevant issues including power cuts as and then they arise.

One might say that I am well and truly a part of the furniture in China. My status as a teacher is most welcome because I am being given more than adequate facilities to fulfil my job competencies. Even if things don't go as planned there should be enough time to figure something out before the next assignment or lesson begins. As of the summer 2018, my teaching adventures have been exposed to: Three Training centers; Two of which were in Jiangsu Province from 2009 to 2010. The other was in Tianjin from 2017 to 2018. One Primary school was in Liaoning Province in 2010. Two High Schools which were in Shanxi Province 2011 to 2012 and Tianjin, 2015 to 2016. One University in Henan Province was from 2012 to 2014. Five Middle schools in Tianjin from 2014 to 2017. One High/Middle school in Beijing which is from 2018 until the present.

Seasonal or Part Time jobs including Summer and Winter periods, have also affected my career. There have been some Private tutorials or Training centres and or when the jobs cropped up.

Summer camps were at: Xiamen in 2010; Hangzhou in 2012; Tianjin in 2015; Yichang in 2016, and Beijing 2018. Winter Camps were in Beijing in 2011, 2014 and 2017 and finally Tianjin in 2015.

So, if I collate my colossal travel and work experiences that includes that of Nepal; 2002 to 2008 and China; 2009 to 2018. All in all, I can calculate an impressive fifteen years in two countries. As you can well imagine I have a pretty good idea of what this type of teaching is all about in addition to my file management system. I am not sure if this is advisable to compare my collection to other teachers but this also includes: Digital pictures, writing, films, documentaries, videos plus legal documents. If one was to add on all the research, organizing and traveling that I have done ever since 1985 it must amount to over thirty years of an unbelievable odyssey. I might also define it as culmination of a Meaning of Life. Another definition of summing up this epic journey in life would be defined something like this:

How many people in this world have lived through the trials of life over a duration of 50 or more years and somehow remained mentally and physically intact? Not so many and so finding a person who can relate to me with a similar background would be a very special occurrence. My lifespan has still been relatively short with under average resources to help me out. At least in the Far East my life has been drastically upgraded and some of the many benefits include being proficient in Microsoft and Apple computers. Regardless of what they say about each system I recommend being able to use both. My teaching profession was carved and created from nothing but guts and determination. Even with the constant changing of legal, political, and educational reforms, it doesn't take much mental ingenuity to wonder will happen next? I now live almost without using liquid cash because most of my finances are executed with my mobile phone. The number of classes per week plus the quantity of students per class will be the main focus in chapter six.

Chapter 6

Number of students/classes

Public Schools/Training Centers

Schools are different so it is apt for change in the place you teach. By far the smallest number of students that I have taught is private tutorials or one to one. As many as 90 people came to some evening classes during my time at a University in Henan Province. So, you see, the difference in numbers are really quite substantial. The majority of public schools will normally give foreigners 20 to twenty-two lessons weekly but rarely more. That works out to be 80 to eighty-four a month. A Training or Language Center give 30 to 40 teaching or office hours. About twelve students attend each class from Grade one to Grade eight. Public schools do change their numbers from week to week. If a training center wants as many as 40 hours a week, that's the equivalent to eight hours a day and five days a week. Even if you have no classes there is a need to be present in the school for the occasional demo classes which have to be performed by the foreigners. It can be all of a sudden, or prepared in advance to attract students to register.

If more than 20 classes per week are requested by the public school, the salary is supposed to be higher. If you have the energy to work at least twenty-five to 30 teaching hours, do accept the offer. If it's too strenuous than you are better off finding a more comfortable and relaxing position. The most I have taught in any one week is twenty-four at a public school in Tianjin. For the salary that I was getting in 2016, that was not suitable. By far the lightest schedule I had was only 4 classes a week at a language center in Tianjin. The salary was significantly higher and much less pressure. Lessons at a public school are normally conducted over a nine-month period excluding the holidays, exams, and social activities. A training center will generally sap up a great deal more of your time over no less than eleven months of the financial year. The hours are not only less convenient plus there are different numbers of students per class. Taking leave for over one week at a training center normally needs a special request at least one month prior and even then it's not guaranteed if you will paid like a normal month.

My very first teaching position was as a co-ordinator in Nepal. I more or less decided how many lessons to do each week. Because of the soothing and pulsating atmosphere, I decided to teach five or six classes per day and six days a week. During some weeks, there were changes due to holidays, strikes, and exams. I was one of a kind in that environment due to loyalty. Even if you work hard in China at a public school or training center, there is still more than enough time to recuperate yourself with the preferred lifestyle. There is always something happening which will affect your teaching at the very last moment. If your lesson is cancelled, sit back and have a cup of tea or coffee plus a piece of cake. The amount of time for teaching can also vary but I will attempt to conclude to the best of my ability what is required: 1) Demo classes range from as little as 10 minutes but on rare occasions it can be even 60 minutes. The reason is because of the demands of the school, parents, and students. Most short demos are not more than 20 minutes. This is designed so the school can see your method and quality. 2) Public school classes can range from 40 to 45 minutes during a normal semester. If it's any more than it's a private institution. I have performed lessons of 40 minutes; 45 minutes; 60 minutes (one hour); 90 minutes or 1 ½ hours; 105 minutes (one hour and forty-five minutes) and 120 minutes (two hours). Lessons of 60 minutes or more require a minimum rest period of 10 minutes to rest.

The number of students per class have averaged out between 20 to 30. If there are less students, it's supposed to be much easier to teach. If there are more than 30 to 40 in the classroom it's very hard to know how to control them. Optimum or preferred numbers of students in any institution school can vary between 10 to 20. I have very good reason to believe that China is projecting on reforms to regulate and control numbers of classes and students. It's not sure how long this process will take to perfect. Modern day China, is certainly a drastic improvement on what used to be a very primitive way of life. Above all, whatever you do in the office and classroom, try to exercise as much flexibility, understanding, and patient as possible. Keep a low profile, do all the tasks which are required, and above all be grateful for what you are doing.

Chapter 7

Making up Classes/Change of Schedule

This is a recap of what I wrote previously in previous chapters. Perhaps the explanation will be easier to absorb plus relevant supplementary information. Make up classes or a change in the schedule happens due to: Public Holidays; periodic and final exams; Social activities (sports, arts, singing, dancing, plays, oral tests, art work, and parents' meetings); There might also be a need to sort out some private affairs such as legalities, medical check-ups or attend some family matters.

In the event of missing classes or schedule changes, this is done any time in the week, weekends or evenings. It depends on the circumstances but it's very rare indeed to make up every single class. I have never once had to catch up on every single lesson which was cancelled or missed. The reason is because the local teachers and students are far too busy with exams, cultural activities or personal affairs. 75 to 95% of all made up classes were either during weekends or evenings. Occasionally, the headmaster will not ask you to make up if it's just for one single lesson or day. The hassle for the local teachers and students to fill in is too much to change the schedule but your salary is still unaffected because this is a part of your contract. If you are suddenly free, take it easy and recover from a busy period. If in the scenario that you are not able to make up for missing classes, your salary might be affected. It's really and truly at the discretion of the school or agent with regards to enforcing their policies with foreigners.

Chapter 8

Overtime

If it does happen, it's mainly at the weekend and very rare indeed. Lessons are paid at time and a half. If you think about it that is quite good because 150RMB for example goes quite a long way at the local supermarket. RMB means Renminbi, it's otherwise known as Yuan which is the currency used in China. Nowadays, most or all payments including overtime are made electronically by bankcard, Alipay, or Wechat. All of my overtime at the same school were performed at the weekend with demos to attract new students. Let's not confuse this with Part time.

Chapter 9

Part time or seasonal work

Most of the full-time contracts are not allowing foreigners to do part time after regular schooling hours. It's breach of contract but foreigners do it so long as its kept a secret. There are those schools that do encourage this to supplement your work load and salary. This can be done during the summer and winter vacations. The payment for part time is at the discretion of the foreigner and person needing the lessons. The range of payment varies between online and directly in person. The lowest amount I received was 40 RMB for one hour using skype or a we-chat video. I have received between 70 to 200 RMB for one hour at someone's private home or training center. The amount to be paid also varies on the cost of living.

Between 2010 and 2017, I was lucky enough to participate in fact finding summer and winter camps. The programs differed between the schools. Most of the agreements normally include food, accommodation and travel expenses depending on the distance that was needed to get there. Since 2012 there has nearly always been an opportunity to do some extra work. If you are free with little or nothing to do than it's a good idea. This will always keep your body and mind busy but it can also be very tiring. The choice is entirely up to you but if you need some extra money, have some fun.

Chapter 10

Public School/Training/Language Centers

In this chapter I will try to focus on any other specific information that was omitted from previous parts of the book with regards to Public Schools and Training Language Centers. Training Centers, are more fussy than Public schools. If they can't benefit financially from you even if you are legal and professional then out, you go. Their overall requirements might include stricter materials. If there are complaints, you will find out sooner or later. A good number of schools offer reasonable salaries, but one of the biggest drawbacks is the irregular schedule. They operate from 3 p.m., to 8.30 on Wednesdays, Thursdays, and Fridays. Some of the adult training centers close as late as 9 p.m. The reason for the late hour is people finish work or studying and are not able to come earlier. Most of the smaller age groups finish no later than 7 or 8 but the staff must remain until 8.30 for additional enquiries. On Saturdays and Sundays, the opening times can vary from 9 in the morning to 7 in the evening.

If a Training Center operates throughout the year with only a handful of rest days the whole year, be very careful of what might be demanded from you. I know that Web International is one of the largest adult training centers in the country. The number of those schools are steadily increasing. The incredible staff turnover for local teachers and foreigners is a negative issue which must raise some alarms bells. If a new branch Sesame Street or Kids Castle, opens up this includes trading during some of the national holidays to attract more business. So, you can understand that the amount of free time which is given at Training Centers is much more limited and varies from place to place. If foreigners don't mind working those hours and preparing lessons according to what is required, it's okay. But a tendency for a very high staff turnover and some customer dissatisfaction remains high on the agenda unless this can be rectified.

Public Schools: are normally much more flexible and lenient with all conditions of work. As long as you do as you are told it's basically coming in for classes at the correct time and going home straight after the last one. Extra curriculum activities, bonuses and facilities depend on the school. International public schools tend to be much stricter with what the students need to learn. If more than five lessons are scheduled per day, take it easy and please don't tire yourself out too much during the morning. If you are invited out to dinner accept the offer gracefully and most of all enjoy yourself. Whatever you decide to do, go where you think your expertise is most beneficial and change if you are not happy.

Chapter 11

Good and bad lessons

In this chapter, I will attempt to explain what can go right or wrong in the classroom. Inexperienced teachers take longer to fathom out the correct or incorrect methods of teaching. Experimentation, judgement, wisdom, and patience are needed to become professional.

Good lessons are when nearly everything that you planned goes according to your wishes. For example: The material is clearly understood by the students and they have a chance to speak at least once or twice; There is a minimal amount of noise generated by the students; The computer systems are fully operational and virus free; A local teacher or class monitors help you to control the class if and when necessary: It's possible to teach an expected amount of material in an allotted amount of time with maybe even a little extra reserved for some fun and games; The amount of energy needed to conduct the class is minimal with plenty left over in time for the next class; The students don't engage in doing their homework or play with any electronic devices in the classroom; The students really do want to learn some information. Other definitions of a good class could be used but I think you can grasp the concept of what I am trying to express.

Bad lessons are when nearly everything that you planned doesn't goes according even to your minimum of requirements. For example: The materials are not suitable for the students and they don't all have a chance to speak at least once: There is a maximum amount of noise generated by the students and some of whom can't keep quiet for a few seconds: The computer system is not fully functional: Even a local teacher or class monitors can't help you to control the class. That might not necessarily be your fault; It's not possible to teach an expected amount of material in an allotted amount of time: No energy or desire in reserve for a game or indeed the next class: The students engage in doing their homework or playing with electronic devices even if they are not permitted to have them in the classroom. The students really can't be bothered to learn; They come late to class and don't even look at any teaching material: They don't really care how you punish them for causing distractions to others; If I want to estimate a percentage of good and bad lessons since I arrived in China, it's a little hard to say: 75% good 25% bad. For me that is maintaining a good average. If something goes wrong I can act accordingly so, in or out of the school before the next lesson begins. Despite my mental and physical strategic approach, it's best not to show off. Being flexible is an important quality needed to maintain my reputation. I am not claiming it's the easiest of careers that I could or would have chosen and preferred. Since October 2002 if we wish to back date my adventures from Nepal it's the only one that I have been able to carve and create virtually out of next to nothing. Not only that but it was achieved at a minimal of costs, energies, desires, and other basic resources.

Chapter 12

Overcoming fatigue

It was only during my teaching program in Nepal, did I realize how mentally and physically this career could be. Interaction, lesson planning, making changes are all mentally and physically tiring not to mention, time consuming. Perhaps Nepal was a little less important due to the obligations and realization of no financial reward in exchange. That didn't exonerate me from performing my duties plus the memoirs from my three visits will never be quite forgotten. The Chinese expect me to do a good job with an over average salary. But like all circumstances, if you feel that your body is overwhelmed by tiredness due to exertion. Try speak in a much lower tone with the aid of a portable speaker or microphone. Don't speak to strongly for prolonged periods of time. Allow the students to speak more if possible. You can also show an educational and entertaining video or movie to calm everyone down including yourself before the class is over. Sing some songs that they are familiar with. If time and space permit, try playing some physical games in the classroom. Even drink some hot liquid to sooth your voice: Grabbing 40 winks during the lunch break if you are really lucky will also allow some time for recovery.

Working in all jobs generally tires you out with some tasks being more strenuous than other. If you are younger than your body will have more energy but exhaustion will still affect your social or personal life as well as subsequent lessons. The most I ever did in one full day was seven. Four in the morning and three in the afternoon. I don't need to remind you how tired I was when I got home. Up to two hours on my bed was needed to recover. Some schools expect foreigners to work 25 to 30 hours a week. Some of my part time jobs required six teaching hours every day for about eight days and no rest in-between. I accepted this without any complaining about mental exhaustion but whatever you do at school, take care of your body.

Chapter 13

Feeling of accomplishments

I do feel rather good after being so long in a teaching career. If I include all the mental, and physical preparation from 2002, I would consider myself to having done phenomenally well. Perhaps other teachers share similar expressions of gratitude. It does feel rather awesome to walk into a school and have the ability to stand in front of students and local teachers before conducting a lesson. But now that I have accomplished this target I am more than satisfied to remain for what might be for the rest of my working life. Opening up my own Training School is one target. That in effect would allow me to employ teachers including foreigners, and register students. Alas, that isn't so realistic because I am lacking funds, an operating license, equipment, and premises. Maybe that or other dreams such as being a famous travel writer will materialize before long and when this is least expected.

Chapter 14

Bonuses, awards, benefits, socializing, opportunities

Being a foreign English teacher is full of bonuses, awards, benefits, and socializing. If I compared this to the life I had in Israel, United Kingdom, America, and Nepal than life is certainly a bed of roses. This is due to: Above average salaries; buying more clothes and IT equipment; Going out to dinner more often; More trips in and out of China especially during exams and paid public holidays: Being invited to dinner parties, weddings, and national holiday celebrations is a chance to be able to absorb some basic Mandarin Chinese. Bonuses are normally given every half a year or at the end of the contract. Travel expenses to cover the airfare normally amount to 8000 RMB or about 800 pounds. Some additional allowances are given during the financial year which includes pocket money, fresh fruit, berries, cakes and if you are really lucky, an invitation to an annual trip which lasts for more than one day.

One trip in 2010 was only half a day in which we visited some botanical gardens in the southern coastal port of Xiamen. Another one was in the same year when I plus another teacher from the same school went to a seaside resort at the Bohai Sea. In the same semester year, the headmaster took us for trip to a temple and dinner. In 2011, another company took all the foreigner teachers and local teachers to an adventure park, dinner party, and a walk up a mountain in Shanxi Province. In the summer of 2012, another school took all the foreigners to one seaside resort in Zhejiang province including dinner.

Another trip was to a majestic waterfall near Yichang in 2016. Most of my other visits in China were accompanied with Yvonne. This included some parts of Beijing which is spread out over a large area. Our very first visit was during National Holiday of 2009. In 2010, we were able to visit the International Expo in Shanghai as well as the delightful city of Wuxi. Another delightful visit was to Yunnan Province in 2012. In the same year, we went to the Zhangjiajie national park in Hunan Province. If I include all my additional long, intermediate and lengthy train journeys for business or pleasure, I must have passed through or visited as many as 25 provinces. That is a quite a lot considering the time scale of just over nine years. Most of the time I have supported Yvonne was earning a much lower salary. Before I came to China, Yvonne hadn't been out of the country, not even to Hong Kong. We managed to visit as many as 6 countries out of China. In 2012, this was the Philippines and Nepal. In 2013, we went to Malaysia. In 2015, Bali graced us with her treasures. In 2016, we went to Thailand. Our last or most recent visit was to the small South Korean Island of Jeju.

If just add to all those wild and wonderful adventures of Danny and Yvonne, I was lucky to receive a few completion contract bonuses from the relevant schools or the agencies. In 2013, Yvonne was allowed to buy an apartment at a subsidized rate in her home town of Wuqing, Tianjin. In 2016/7, Yvonne was finally able to buy a car for the first time in her life. Prior to that she passed her driving test. At the beginning of the winter in 2017, I was successful in achieving just over the minimum pass mark in a theory test to enable me to get a legal Chinese driving license for the first time. That in effect gives us the freedom and luxury on the roads without having to rely on a bus or train.

In 2017/2018 we bought a flat with a joint agreement in the seaside resort of Qinhuadao, Hebei Province. There is still some debt incurred of $100,000 to one of the banks with a monthly mortgage of 4200 RMB for 10 years. We both have international credit cards facilities which were approved by a joint ownership from the Bank of China and Air China respectively. During the last two to three years most of our payments for basic products are done online or by using Alipay or Wechat. It goes without saying that the use of liquid cash is rapidly going out of fashion much sooner than originally thought. For an experienced teacher, the monthly salaries for oral or conversational English can range from 10,000 to 15,000 RMB after tax with a free flat or accommodation. If you are offered between 15,000 to 20,000 RMB, before tax, then you will only get a rental subsidy because the area is quite expensive. If the agency or school wants to pay less, think twice before accepting the job.

Chapter 15

Accommodation and project renewal

Where-ever you are staying in China you need somewhere to live. Buying or renting property differs according to the area, age, size and overall quality of the building. Over the last 50 years the government has modernized large parts of the country including those citizens who live in the more rural areas. As much as 700 million people were believed to be living in a state of poverty or one step away above it. That has been drastically reduced in the last 20 years with many changes including project renewals. Foreign teachers need a place to live when working for a school. If the school wishes to save money they will offer you a dormitory in the school. Alternatively, they can rent out a flat which is quite close. This can be done by sharing with another foreigner or alone. When you sign an agreement, try to make sure what you wish or prefer to do. It's always possible to negotiate but that might also affect your salary, yearly bonus and other small benefits. It's basically anything to economize. The walking distance should be within no more than fifteen to twenty minutes from the school at the very most. If public transportation is needed than it might be advisable to buy an electric or push bicycle. With regards to utilities such as: Water, power, heating, gas, internet and sometimes cleaning. The company or school might be willing to pay everything but at the expense of a smaller salary. If you need to pay only for the water, power, gas, and cleaning it doesn't matter so much. Some schools even offer a small monthly allowance for utilities. Most apartments should include some furniture, cooking equipment, central heating, TV, a wardrobe for clothes, air conditioning, washing machine, electric cooker or gas stove, fridge, boiler or solar panels for hot water. They should also provide a water machine for drinking and some linen for the bedroom. If the salary is much higher than you need to pay for everything else including: Agency fee, three months' rent in advance, one month's deposit and all the bills. Depending on the area it's really quite expensive and not so convenient. Each time you take leave, the landlord still needs to be paid for the rent while you cover all the bills. My recommendation from personal experience is to negotiate a free flat, because its much less hassle and will lead to relative peace of mind. Be careful with the conditions of the contract which can be subject to change from time to time. If for whatever reason you are not satisfied there will be a need to consider changing your boss within 90 days from the expiration date of your visa.

Chapter 16

Changing or keeping bosses

When you work with an agency or school it's a good idea to remain there for as long as possible rather than change every one or two years. I have been rather unfortunate in this respect to have moved around more times than what I actually preferred. Three of the main reasons was the suitability, reliability and honesty of the school, agency, or even other foreigners. If, in the event that you feel something is wrong, your services are being used for marketing. Having white skin, a British passport and accent still indicates a distinct advantage. The same is true for Americans, Canadians, Australians, and New Zealanders. Trying to be within the legal working age also attracts schools or agencies to hiring you. It used to be up to fifty-five in some provinces while most accept you even up to the age of 60. Some schools especially those with younger students prefer female or male graduates. The reason is to attract more children so the school gets richer. I must admit that leaving or changing jobs was not so convenient in terms of needing to remain legal or financially stable. You can forfeit a bonus if you need to leave early or the boss is not happy. Please don't place the entire blame on you because this is wasted energy. I wasn't happy in the slightest about resettling so many times but there are situations which were well out of my control. A school or agency wishes to keep or change you for economic reason or to show a new face to students even if your lessons are interesting.

If you can remain for at least two years or four semesters in a job than try to negotiate a better salary and living conditions. Training centers have higher staff turnover because of inadequate conditions of work, accommodation and sometimes lower salaries. Whatever situation arises with the new visa policies which began in 2017, I would recommend 90 days to be the minimum requirement needed for renewal or termination of your contract. If you wish or need to leave for whatever reason than ask for the required documentation, leaving salary and completion bonus if applicable. If you can remain longer it will give you more time to sort yourself out later on. Some foreigners prefer changing jobs because they are not satisfied with the original agreement. The leaders often change their minds with regards to the conditions of work. Long hours, inadequate IT equipment, poor accommodation, and certainly no health insurance. Sometimes you are hired because the school is in such an awful rush to get a foreigner. If that happens, consider yourself to be lucky. As a matter fact, it happened to me at least once, and gave me and the school more time to sort ourselves out. The longer you remain in China, money will keep coming in and you will enjoy the many perks of living and working and remain legal at the same time.

Chapter 17

Please try to remain legal

Being legal is by far the most integral aspect of all when visiting any foreign country. If for whatever reason you break or misunderstand the law, there might very well be fines to pay. Depending on the seriousness of the offense you could face a period of imprisonment and in some circumstances even extradition. Excuses of; I didn't know or am ignorant are not normally tolerated by any police in any country. In any event, try not to bribe the police officer to leave you alone because unless they are really greedy for money, that might not be acceptable. In 2009, China despite all her external and internal problems welcomed foreigners for business and pleasure purposes. It was a basically a situation of doing more or less what you wanted without anyone bothering to check up. As you can imagine, the law was being broken left right and center by many foreigners, Chinese nationals and companies in China. Due to the size of the total land mass and population, tracking down offenders was a little difficult. Even if a suspect was caught, evidence was still required to make a conviction.

A basic tourist or travel visa lasts 30 days and was very easy to obtain in 2009. Filling out an application form, handing in your passport at the local embassy and waiting for three to four working days to get the approval was all that it took. You kept the receipt and upon returning to the consulate, payment was made in exchange for your passport. Other types of visas were a bit more complicated but included; Business, Family, Work, Student, Pilot, Journalist, and Permanent. The cost of visas depended on how much processing was needed. There was a list of relevant or required original documents according to the nationalities, and how many entries are needed. A single entry was normally the most common and cheapest. A double entry was more expensive. Multi-entry visas were the most expensive but gave you much more flexibility. From my understanding, most foreigners who came to China in 2009, even with a job offer applied for a Business Visa or F category. 90 days was the initial duration with the possibility of extending this for an additional 90 or 180 days. No more than 360 days or one year were allowed before it was necessary to leave the country and reapply for the same category from your country of origin. I do know that a large number of foreigners kept coming and leaving China on Business visas without officially applying for a legal Working Visa. Getting approved for a legal Working Visa or Z category in or out of China was more complicated. The documentation used to include: A recommendation letter from your previous boss, health check, bachelor's degree, TEFL or teaching certificate, a registration card or proof of address from the local police station in your area. The majority of foreigners preferred to do this from within the mainland but a business trip to Hong Kong to get those initial exit and entry stamps plus visa stamp in your passport was still obligatory. Tourist, Student and Business Visas from

2009 to 2013 could be changed into Working Visas during this period. If you were already in China on a Business Visa, then your boss would get the relevant documents from the local or nearest Foreign Expert Bureau in the provincial capital for a Working or (Z) Visa. Once the documents were approved you could set about going to Hong Kong to get this stamped in your passport. A validity of 30 days was than more than enough time to change it to a yearly Resident Permit stamp back in the mainland. To get the Resident Permit you needed firstly to obtain what was known as a F.E.C or Foreign Experts Certificate. It came in the form of a small blue Booklet which was also obtained at the Foreign Expert Bureau. There were a few pages, one of which had your main details plus a special number. Extra pages were provided for additional stamps when renewal was necessary. Once the F.E.C had been issued or stamped, the rest of the application process was very easy.

Your very first time in the city or province would require your boss would take you, your health certificate, your passport, two pictures and the legal documentation from the company to the last stage of the visa process. It was called the PSB, Public Security Bureau or Entry and Exit Bureau. All immigration officers are obligated to issue foreigners with new Visas, or Visa Renewals. Not every foreigner applies for the same category because they don't all work. The validity of the Work Visa or Resident Permit used to be according to the contract or F.E.C. Before the passport was submitted, a picture was also taken as evidence that you are who you are. Payment was then executed after which you were given a receipt. Even though the actually processing time for each application takes a few minutes but your passport is in a waiting list for about eight working days. If it takes any longer than there are many more foreigners who are waiting the same facility. Only you or your agent is allowed to collect your passport in exchange for the receipt. This was one of the most common and easiest ways to get legal in China. It also permitted foreigners to live a comfortable life and enjoy the treasures from the Far East.

I was also under the distinct impression that private companies were also offering to process Working Visas. Just how legitimate they were remained to be seen, not to mention the cost, convenience or honesty. It wasn't even certain if they had associates with the correct government officials. I don't really recommend this method because its taking one hell of a risk. They might say processing time is much faster and will obtain any missing paperwork if necessary. This method might also be illegal let alone the cost. Above all, try to keep to the normal way of using the Foreign Expert Bureau and Public Security Bureau as means of leaving or entering the country.

It has also come to my attention that a large number of foreigners are still working or intent on get work on Tourist, Business, Student, and Marriage Visas. They know that it's not allowed but they still do it. If people decided to take the risk, it is up to their discretion if the authorities decide to check up on foreigners. From September 2009 to the beginning of March 2011, I was participating on what was called Cultural Exchange Programs. That was perfectly legal. The next important topic which needs to be discussed is the so called high or low risk categories:

A so called High Risk area were the larger cities such as Beijing, Shanghai, Guangzhou, Tianjin or Shenzhen. The population was between 10 to 20 million. Visa or documentation checks were much more frequent because of additional availability of manpower. A Low Risk area was more rural. Legality checks were much less because the local authorities simply couldn't be bothered to implement basic governmental procedures. The salaries in low risk areas were much less than high risk areas. Making that decision where to go to work was entirely up to you. However, in many of the high-risk areas, foreigners were causing many self-inflicted problems. Some examples were, doing business on the wrong visa, dealing with drugs, causing breach of the peace. Causing damage to property or people. Having sex with people who are below the legal age of sixteen. In the low risk areas, the crime rate was much lower or it simply wasn't publicised. If you got caught, the consequences were potentially devastating.

2011, was the year that I got my first legal working approved for Shanxi Province Central China. The visa was only valid for that province and nowhere else. Each province had her own state policy so if you wished to transfer, a new visa had to be approved and processed with a recommended time scale of 30 to 60 days. In Shanxi Province, a monthly salary of only 5500 RMB was offered plus free accommodation, heating, internet and a yearly bonus of 7000 RMB. Additional documents needed for the transfer in (2012) was a recommendation letter from my company and full medical check. The recommendation letter was not just a normal letter which anyone could prepare. It had to be a standard governmental format by the school plus an official red stamp or seal from the HR. My reason for moving to Henan Province was I hoped would be an improved salary and social life, compared to my previous position. Once my passport had been processed, the work began and lasted until January 2014. For a time, I was content and there were some part time positions such as private tutorials, Saturday afternoons at another university, and finally a kindergarten. I wasn't supposed to do it but as long as I kept it quiet, everything would be fine.

If I excluded my part time, it was possible to calculate that on a yearly basic my average monthly salary was not more than 5500 RMB. That was no improvement but it was enough to remain legal. Being far from Yvonne was another issue before I decided to move to Tianjin. A larger salary was offered but the cost of living was higher. Seeing Yvonne was nice from time to time but the social life was not better. Being legal was still my main issue so I decided to be happy with what I had. During the next four and half years (January 2014 to May 2018, I had four main bosses and some part time positions. On most occasions when I moved, the visa rules got stricter and stricter. This happened to rid the poor-quality workers or those who were breaking the law. Extra documents were needed. One of which was something called a Cancellation Certificate. This indicated that the local government cancelled your old work visa number from your old boss but it didn't cancel your Resident Permit stamp in your passport. A new number could be issued by the government before the next visa stamp was given. This rule had been introduced so teachers were not able to move from job to job as they so pleased. It wasn't long before every province in China required such a letter and it could only be prepared at the Foreign Expert Bureau. If no such letter was prepared and processed, the visa couldn't be renewed. Any planned overseas travel was recommended only after your passport was processed. The next two documents were a Medical check and Recommendation letter which was very easy indeed. As long as you were on good relations with the school that could be prepared in the HR office. The medical document needed to be prepared by a certified hospital. A Non-Criminal Statement was also being introduced to prove that you had no addiction to drugs, no grievous bodily harm and had not molested Chinese nationals under the age of sixteen. The school could do this with the help of an official police stamp or seal. Going to your country of origin was not necessary. The very last document which needed to be prepared by the school was a Discharge letter. This stipulated and proved that you had worked from certain dates for the last company and they had now released you from their employment.

In 2016 there was yet another major change in which some provinces and cities started to ask for a verification letter or seal of University Diplomas. This was especially true if you were applying for a legal Working Visa for the first time or a transfer to some provinces. As you see, a lot depended on how strict the local government or school was. If you stayed in the same province no such verification was needed. Not only that but it wasn't just enough to get this verification from a local agent as some people were doing. The Chinese government had to stamp it with an official seal. So, life was getting very stringent with a number of foreigners being severely restricted. By the year 2017 it was almost impossible for any foreigner to apply for a working visa directly from Hong Kong. The normal process, if this was your first time, needed to begin in your country of origin. For those who had working visas it was still possible to renew so long as you had all the necessary documents. In the same year, as if this wasn't so hard already, the government preferred that only those foreigners coming from native English speaking countries. If you were colored from a Non-English speaking country, it was much harder for schools to process a working visa. Not only that but colored people especially Negros were subjected to extra interrogations with regards to their purpose for visiting China. Those who originated from: United Kingdom, United States, Canada, Australia, and New Zealand were normally left alone on the assumption that you were legal and weren't trouble makers. The next requirement for processing a visa was having a TEFL or Teaching Certificate which had a minimum of 120 learning hours. The quantity of new regulations as well as the new variety of visas which were now being issued by the Chinese Embassy was amazing but not surprising.

The last change that I know about came about on 1st April 2017. The Foreign Expert Bureau begun a system which affected all working visas. The blue booklet or Foreign Expert Certificate was in affect shut down on the 30th June 2017. That left only 90 days for foreigners to transfer the old visas to the new ones without any hassle. If you were too late it was necessary to begin the whole process again. Three main categories of work visa were now implemented which also went according to a special points system.

A-visas were only issued to professors at universities; businessman, or multi-million entrepreneurs. The minimum number of points needed were eight-five. Only a very small minority of people could get this visa but at an anticipated minimum monthly salary of 30,000 to 50,000 RMB. It also depended on how old you were, how many years of practical teaching experience you had, what diploma you had and the level of your Chinese.

B-visas were issued to the majority of foreign English teachers. The basic legal requirements were a minimum of 60 points. That also included at least two years of practical teaching experience, Masters and Bachelors Diplomas, a certain level of Chinese and not being more than 60 years old. The average salary for this category was between 10,000 to 15,000 to 20,000 RMB.

C-visas were issued for just below 60 points. Normal industrial workers were entitled to get this but a University Diploma was not a requirement. Salaries were lower as were the conditions of work.

To get the new work permit or a Foreigner's ID card, all documentation needs to be uploaded onto an online system for approval by the SAFEA or State Administration of Foreign Experts Affairs. The processing time depending on the city, can now take between five to 10 working days. Your boss will then take the approval and apply in person for the Work Permit card at the same place. It takes an additional five to 10 days to process after which your boss takes you, your passport and all the company documentation for processing at the Exit and Entry Bureau or PSB. Processing takes a minimum of seven to 10 days or depending on how many people are in front of you.

I am much happier to confirm that I was approved with a B category or new Working Visa in July 2017. That indicates having a permanent foreigner's Identity Card. Of course, it's not the same as a Chinese National ID card but once your details are confirmed on the system there is really no need to be concerned about being legal. The information on your work permit relates to the, province where you are working, your name, passport number, employer, residential address, and validity of the visa. Renewing or transferring a new work visa is very simple indeed but the recommended processing time is normally between 30 to 50 days.

If you are renewing, the only original documents that are needed are, a new contract from your boss which will be signed and stamped plus submitting your passport. For transfers to a new city or province, the following documentation are needed: 1) Company Release; 2) Government Cancellation; 3) Recommendation; 4) Stamped and signed Contract and Legal documents from your boss. A medical certification is depended on the company. University Diploma Verifications and Non-Criminal Checks are not necessary. If you are not sure what the procedure is than contact your local Chinese Embassy in your country of origin if you are out of China. If you are in China, verify with the person in charge of Foreign Affairs at your school or company. I sincerely hope that this chapter can be helpful and you can abide by the rules and regulations of working in China.

Chapter 18

Job Description/Sample Contract

There are many types of job descriptions and contracts.

This is just one sample of a job description

I am not obligating you to read it from start to finish but it's just to make you aware of how it looks.

Job Description

Native English Teacher required in Fuzhou 11,000- 13,000 plus housing allowance of 2000 RMB per month.

1.) Candidate Requirements

    1.1   Native English Speaker from the USA, UK, AUS, CANADA, and NEW ZEALAND.

    1.2   Demonstration of a neutral accent, clear pronunciation, and English rhythm.

    1.3   Minimum of a bachelor's degree (masters preferred) plus Chinese legalized.

    1.4   Proof of no criminal background check (Chinese legalized)

    1.5   TESOL/TEFL/CELTA

    1.6   A minimum of 2-years teaching experience with reference letters.

2.) Position description

    2.1   2.1 Age of students: 18 to 25

    2.2   2.2 Number of students per class: about 30

    2.3   2.3 Each classroom is equipped with a computer, projector, microphone and speakers.

    2.4   2.4 Curriculum provided by Australian and American Universities

    2.5   2.5 Teachers are responsible for developing and contributing to the existing curriculum, constructing lesson plans, partaking in scheduled meetings and keeping detailed records of their work and work of their students.

3.) Remuneration and Benefits

    3.1   Monday to Fridays (no nights)

    3.2   Salary 11,000- 13,000, negotiable based on previous experience,   education, and credentials.

    3.3   Insurance: Domestic Medical Insurance Provided

    3.4   Air fare or contraction completion bonus: 8000 RMB yearly Airfare allowance

    3.5   Off campus accommodation allowance provided to the amount of 2000

    3.6   Work Permit/ID card/Resident Permit provided

    3.7   18 Hours of teaching and five hours of administration per week

4.) Working location

Fuzhou Melbourne University, University town, Fuzhou City, Fuzhou Province.

5.) About Fuzhou Melbourne University

FMU is an international institution tertiary education which is an Outcome from the cooperation from Minjiang University and Public Universities overseas. The international cooperation of which dates back to the Sino-Aus Cooperation for high level vocational talents in 1999 and 2000. So far FMU has been the only Sino-Foreign Cooperative Institution approved by the ministry of education in Fujian Province as a completely independent foreign cooperative School. It is also a window and platform for the International Exchange and cooperation that begins with the Minjiang University.

6.) About China Liberal

China Liberal Education Technology (Beijing Ltd), Company (China Liberal) as a comprehensive education company, specialized in Sino Foreign cooperative education foreign talents introducing and online Platform R & D, is fully backed by over 10 -year related experience And capital investment of 12.8 million HKD. At present cooperating with domestic colleges and universities, we have set up seven Sino- cooperative academies which prove we have the experience and ability to introduce and integrate rich foreign high quality educational resources and well as cooperation with colleges and universities home and abroad to develop international educational programs on the aspects of education operation management service, investment and so on....

The most recent contract that I have signed was with a company based in Beijing in 2018. This is standard procedure to working and living in China.

Foreign Staffer's Employment Contract

Party A: Beijing Enke Education Technology CO., LTD
Party B: Daniel Teller (should be hand written signature)

ESL TEACHER CONTRACT

The parties to this contract are: Beijing Enke Education Technology CO., LTD herein called "the Employer".and Daniel Teller herein called "the Employee". And it is made with reference to the following

Employer (Party A)
Name of the Employer: Beijing Enke Education Technology CO., LTD.
Legal Representative: Ying Quan.
Address: Room 1906, Building D2, Tian Chuang Shi Yuan, No 21, Da Tun Road, Chaoyang District, Beijing, China- Tel- 010-52420172,
Fax: 010- 64801391

Employed Foreign Experts or Professional (Party B)
Name: Daniel Teller
Sex: Male
Date of Birth: 02/06/1964
Nationality: British
ID Number: 511444966
Overseas address: (should be handwritten) 37, Donnington Court, Donnington Road, Willesden, London, NW10 3TG.
Telephone: 00442084518926

This contract is subject to comply with future changes to local labour laws, when the local labour laws are not addressing terms, this contract will prevail.

The Employee is a qualified and experienced and has applied to the school for employment as Employee.

The Employee and Employer have agreed on the following terms of contract.

Term:

The term of this contract is for one year commencing May 1st 2018 and continuing until June 15 2019. The Employee will be subject to a one month probation period during which his contract may be terminated in accordance with the section titled termination.

Employer's duties:

1. The employer will assist the employee with the related procedure.

2. The employer will introduce the employee to his/her own work system and regulations and conduct all direction and supervision and evaluation of the employee's work.

3. The employer will provide a suitable working environment for the employee.

4. The employer will be responsible for paying the salary to the employee.

Employee's Duties

1. The Employee will comply with the laws of the People's Republic of China and will follow the regulations of the schools and company.

2. The information in the Employee's Curriculum Vitae, Resume and References together with any other information submitted to the Employer in support of the Employee's application for employment are true and not misleading in any way.

3. The Employee warrants that he/she is of sound mind and in good physical health. The employee with perform the duties of his/her employment in a professional and diligent manner, and will devote his/her full working time and attention to the duties of his/her employment.

4. The Employee must not harm the image of the employer or fellow workers by his/her conduct and no alcohol during the working time should be consumed.

5. Teaching the contracted working hours and overtime teaching hours in a responsible manner.

6. Finishing the arranged teaching tasks from school supervising tests and exams as well as curriculum development, submitting lesson plans at the start of each working day to the Employer's appointed representative a week before.

7. Assisting with administration including intake and placement of students, counselling students and recording attendance. Once the attendance is recorded the school should be notified by the employee as soon as possible.

8. Participate in the necessary social activities required by schools and company as well as administrative meetings and the employee training programs and demo classes.

9. The employee should take the responsibility for their safety during the holidays, if there is an accident or life safety issue during the traveling, the employer does not bear any responsibility for this.

Payment:

The Employee's payment will consist of the following. Salary will be paid according to the scale.

1. The salary is 11000 RMB per month with free or shared apartment,

2. Salary will be paid on the 10th of each month.

Visa:

When applying for the work Visa, the employer is responsible for the foreign expert license fee, the teacher is responsible for his/own visa fee, medical examination fee, and photographs. If the employee is not qualified for teaching, the employer will bear 50% extra fee for the working fee while the employee should pay for the rest.

When applying for the business visa or student visa the teacher or employee is responsible for his/her own visa fee,

Termination:

1. If either party wishes to terminate the contract before the agreed date, it must give notice in writing to the other party 30 days in advance, otherwise it will compensate the other party to the amount of one month's salary as referred to in section titled "Payment".

2. The Employer reserves the right to terminate the Employee's employment without any severances benefits in the following circumstances:

3. The Employee brings the school into disrepute by his/her conduct or attire.

4. If the Employee is guilty of dereliction of duty, incompetence, insubordination, dishonesty or other breaches of the employee's obligations under this agreement or the rules and regulations of the school.

5. The Employee receives complaints from 50% of the students about his/her teaching quality in two or more classes, AND if the complaints are recognized by the management as reasonable.

6. If the employee cannot satisfy the students or clients the employee is assigned to, and the employer cannot place the employee in more suitable employment.

Safety:

1. For safety reasons, the Teacher is not allowed to do part-time teaching elsewhere unless agreed by the school. Once the teacher does so, the school will verbally warn the teacher. If the teacher ignores the warning and keeps doing so, the school will terminate the contract right away.

2. At the beginning of the semester, the Teacher may attend training courses arranged by the school, to get around the school, status of teachers and student curriculum, as well as the school's rules and regulations. After training, the teacher shall make the teaching plan according to the text book and student levels. The Teacher shall send the next week teaching plan to his/her customer service conductor.

3. For safety, the teacher can travel on weekends and public holidays. This can also be in the weekday for visa renewal, however, he or she shall inform the school or company. While traveling the teacher should be safety conscious, and return to the school on time. The teacher will take all responsibility for any accident happening during the traveling.

4. For safety, the teacher will turn off the power while showering, lock the door when going outdoors, pay attention to valuables, close the gas value after cooking, pay attention to electrical safety, otherwise he or she will take full responsibility for any accidents.

5. For safety, the Teacher shall not drink too much, shall not eat at small restaurants that do not meet health standards, shall not bring a stranger to his or her apartment, shall not ride motor vehicles, otherwise he or she will take full responsibility of any accidents. The teacher shall return to the school or apartment no later than 11 p.m. If there is any special arrangement, he or she shall notify the school or company well in advance.

Apartment:

The apartment is provided by Party A, but Party B will pay for water and electricity, monthly telephone bill, and internet connection service charges and property management fee for each month. Party A will check such amounts at the end of each month, all amounts shall be deducted from Party's B at his/her own expense.

Force Majeure:

In the unlikely event of a disaster such as earthquake, fire, flood, civil unrest, etc. which would make the employer unable to continue operating the business, the contract will be considered void and both parties are released for this contract without any penalties.

Confidentiality:

1. The Employee will not disclose details of his/her salary to any person or party whatsoever.

2. The employee will keep all information about the employer's teaching method and administration confidential.

3. The employee will not use the employer's teaching methods and materials for instruction of any private and/or with another employer.

No poaching

The employee agrees not to approach any of the employer's clients, students, staff and business associates on behalf of another organization for a period of 2 years after leaving the Employer's service. The Employee agrees to compensate the Employer for all losses doubly caused by violation of this clause or be sued to the court.

Breach of Contract:

Either of the two parties fails to fulfil his contract, RMB 6,000 should paid to the other as a penalty for breach of contract.

Leave:

If party B has to ask for personal leave during work time, he/she must obtain the permission from the school and company. And the absent days which incur a deduction. If party B neglects the work to leave without any reason or asking from the school, Party A shall have the right to fine Party B double of his salary during those neglecting days. If party B has been neglecting the work for a continuous period of three days, Party A has the right to terminate cooperation.

Renewal of Contract

Should the Employee desire to renew this contract, he/she should formally make the request no later than one month prior to the termination date of this contract.

Regulations:

The teacher agrees to Respect Chinese culture

1. As a guest, please refrain from behaviour that may cause offense.
2. Be punctual to all classes
3. Be in a fit state to teach, unaffected by drinking or late nights.
4. Not to have romantic/sexual relationships with any students in the Education Centre.
5. Dress well and cleanly. Suits and ties are not required but you are representing the Education Center so please take your lead from the Chinese Staff.
6. Refrain from proselytizing about religion or politics in class.
7. Be considerate of other members of staff in whose culture might well be different from the Teacher's.
8. Each party will receive a signed copy of this contract. Both versions are identical and equal to the eyes of the law.

The Employer   The Employee
Beijing Enke Education Technology CO., LTD...   ... Daniel Teller

Employer's Signature: Rita Xu (handwritten)
Date: March, 30th 2018... 30/03/2018

Please note that an official seal must accompany to validate it otherwise the Foreign Expert Bureau will not accept it. Three copies are made: One is for the government, one for the company and one for the teacher. Refer to the information in case there might be any future discrepancies or misunderstandings. The dates on the contract are clearly stipulated. Of course, there might be additional details that can be checked and verified but the first year is the most important. If a second contract is signed and stamped, one would hope the conditions would improve.

Chapter 19

Danny and Yvonne

Our friendship or just being together has been subject to a lot of cultural changes and adjustments. Perhaps emotional and physical stress can be used to define a part of it. Our different mentalities and educational upbringing has played a part of the development. So, to put everything into the proper prospectus. I experienced what were defined as being predominately proper dwellings in England, Israel America, and to some extent, China. Yvonne had grown up in a small village only until the age of seventeen when she made a big move to the city. As recently as 2013, the local government allowed her to move into a spanking new apartment in Wuqing District, Tianjin, where she still lives today. Because we are so different we try our very best to complement each other for better or for worse. Not wishing to add to the family was a mutual consent based on the understanding that we are well past that period. Despite some instability since we met in China it was necessary to decide on: which jobs to take; where to travel on holidays; eating out; buying clothes, purchasing another apartment, purchasing IT equipment plus much more. It goes without saying that without all morale and financial guidance between us we wouldn't have been able to accomplish so much in a short time. Naturally, I am eternally grateful for this living style in what is not the easiest part of the world to live in. It is sincerely hoped that we can remain humble friends for the rest of our natural days in this world.

Chapter 20

Chinese food (chopsticks)

Eating in your home or a restaurant can be a lot of fun. It depends on what you wish to put inside your body. The variety of good quality products in China are in abundance. From a western cultural point of view, there are types of preferred places to eat your desired food products but the prices and variety maybe a little off-putting. I don't mind eating the food so long I remain fit and healthy. Street sellers or kiosks are just about everywhere but I would think twice before buying one of the many products on offer. Frying eggs, congee, frying dough, fried or boiled dumplings, deep fried pastries which are then filled with chicken or pork sausages and eggs. Some pastries are just baked and filled with vegetables, doujiang or soya milk, noodles; bean drinks, sticks laden with tomatoes, pieces of oranges and covered in caramel or burnt sugar.

Some of those are healthier than others but a trip to the local supermarket is not too hard to accomplish. There are more than ample restaurants which cater for your personal choice with affordable prices. Chopsticks are two long thin sticks which people have been using for eating quite a long time. I don't have a fetish for using them because I originate from the West. If I have no choice I will eat with them but I would prefer, a knife, fork, and spoon. This indicates that I don't wish to delete some of the cultural habits which are still a part of me. So, absorbing in any multicultural society can be done and once you are feeling comfortable you can fine eternal peace with whoever is closest to you.

Chapter 21

Speaking Chinese

Before coming to China, I didn't know even one single word of Mandarin Chinese. Absorbing any part of this dialect was much harder than I could have possibly expected. My linguistic talents which were brought from exploits in other countries was simply massive. To some extent, I am classified as being polylingual or capable of speaking or understanding five or more languages. The degree of fluency varies a great deal. The Chinese dialect was one of the most difficult I have tried to absorb so far. Yvonne enabled me to recognize and even write some of the many syllables. That was quite good for me due to my age. Depending on the conversation and the speed, I can understand quite a lot of basic words and phrases. The language is also written down in a sort of Ping Ying fashion by using the A to Z alphabet. There are also four tones which confuse me and other foreigners who come here. Those who can absorb it should receive a pat of congratulations on the back. As with many other languages, slight changes in tones, letters, and syllables affect the meaning of the words. If I try to speak even some basic Chinese, people will probably not understand me. I am okay with some daily phrases and numbers but most foreigners can absorb this quite easily.

Chapter 22

Dealing with emergencies: Legal, money, and health

This can happen to rich and poor people at anytime, anywhere. The real culprit behind this is based on influence from dishonesty or evil habits. We have all dealt with some of these issues from time to time in our lives. It's not always our fault but we have to cope with the situation as best we know how. In a Non-English speaking country like China which is still undergoing development, it's hard to avoid getting into some form of mischief even if your intentions were admirable. It's hard to know how honest or reliable people are so without going into too much detail. If you are after an adventure perhaps something will go wrong. Depending on the type of problem will test your ability to solve the issues. I have been through some minor and moderate horror stories in my life including China. Though I decline to elaborate on explicit details, many related stories are readable online from expat forums. Alternatively, you might meet someone who will tell you about a horror story which happened to them or someone else. Just be careful in how you live and who you associate with, for business or pleasure. If you can't make the right choice in dealing with a potential or real emergency, then seek some advice from your closest friends. They might be able to help or you just have to try and figure it out alone and hope for the best. Money, legality, betrayal, immigration documents, false promises, misinterpretation, and housing, normally come top of the list. Please try to abide to the best of your ability with the regulations which will pave the route for a happy and eventful stay.

Chapter 23

Your general mental and physical health

Being healthy is always of primary importance. Getting ill can happen to anyone at any time. I must confess to getting ill a number of times in China due to self-inflicting negligence upon myself. Most of the problems were associated with: The common cold, sore throats, tooth aches, stomach aches, fever and back pain. You should know your body better than anyone else. If something goes wrong, try to deal with the matter rather than delay it. If you lose your vocal cords or what is known as laryngitis, take medicine which is available in most chemist shops. They are inexpensive and will help your voice to return to normal. On the whole I have been lucky in context of life-threatening illnesses. As I approach my 55th birthday in 2019, being careful with how I treat mental and physical body is of greater importance than ever before.

Chapter 24

This is now my country for ever and ever

Getting approval for a Permanent Residency Visa or D category is very hard. One of my reasons for emigrating to China was trying to make it a permanent home. The fact is that I came here to use my skills as a Foreign Expert for the benefit of students of all ages was purely coincidental. The thought had also occurred to me for a long time by emigrating to native English speaking countries like, America, Canada, Australia, and New Zealand. Because I am now in my mid 50s, the likelihood of this development happening is become increasingly unrealistic. The reason is due to less demand for ESL teachers in those parts of the world. Seeing as I am in China I might as well remain for good. In 2019, if all goes well I would like to apply for Permanent Residency. One of the most common methods to apply is by right of being married for at least five years to a Chinese National. Other criteria relate to ownership of property and maybe also proof of tax payments to the local government.

The other main reason why I wish to remain here is to be settled in one country for the remainder of my natural life and not wander like a nomadic tribesman. From my previous exploits in the world, no other country or citizens have offered me more in such a short period of time than China. New country, career, international credit card, legalized driving license, advanced travel card on high speed trains, published writer and I am process of buying a new apartment. That I believe just about concludes quite a lot of my current adventures in the People's Republic of China. My story is not unlike other foreigners who come and settle down permanently. For those who have been patient to read this book I hope to meet up with you one fine day and share some other invaluable adventures from time and memorial.

Epilogue/Additional Comments

The exploits for which you have just learnt about, do summarize a certain portion of my life. Even though the government blocked many websites including Facebook, Twitter and YouTube, VPNs can be purchased to access all the popular social media. Any additional omissions might not be relevant to me personally and if necessary do some research online to find out what you need to know. The majority of foreigners in China are able to relate to what I have just written. Those who are planning on coming for business or pleasure, this book is a good insight as to what to expect or more importantly what not to expect from the country or the people. Once you arrive in China, not only is it yours for asking and sharing but try to respect and appreciate all what is being offered to you. Who knows this might very well, lead on to another opportunity which might otherwise, never have presented itself to you on a plate. Dear reader, come and find out what living in China from a multicultural point of view is all about. I will be more than delighted to indulge a list of invaluable treasures from the Far East as you probably never saw them before.

Our sincere gratitude, once again for sharing these and what we hope to be many other pulsating memoirs for the good of mankind.

Danny Teller and Yvonne Wu.

Danny in 2010 in a Primary School in North East China

Danny in a Middle School in 2009, near Tianjin in North East China

*Danny in the same Middle school in 2009,
Tianjin in North East China*

*Danny in a Language Center in Wuqing District,
Tianjin performing in a Halloween party in 2016*

*Danny just outside a Primary School
in North East China in 2010*

Group of teachers near a waterfall in Yichang,
Hubei Province, Central China in 2016

Danny and a teacher during a summer camp
in Yichang, Hubei Province in 2016

Danny and Yvonne at the Shaolin Temple in
Henan Province, 2013, Central China

Danny and some Chinese teachers in a summer camp in Yichang, 2016

Danny and two university students from Ping Ding Shan, 2012, Henan Province, Central China

Danny in Wuqing district, Tianjin North East China

Danny and Yvonne near a seaside resort, Qinhuangdao, Hebei Province, 2016

Students in Ping Ding Shan, Henan Province, 2012

Danny and Yvonne in a flower garden in Qinhuangdao, Hebei Province 2016

Two students from Ping Ding Shan, Henan Province

Danny in Sichuan Province in 2012 near a river

Danny in Beijing, 2016 near some mountains

Nice trees and bushes in Wuqing District, Tianjin in 2016

Danny and a teacher on a boat trip in Sichuan Province, 2012

Gate of Heavenly Peace and the Forbidden City near Central Beijing in 2018

*Danny on a boat next a huge statue of
Buddha in Leshan, Sichuan Province*

*Foreign teachers in Hangzhou, Zhejiang
Province for a summer camp in 2012*

Danny standing near a river in Hangzhou Province, 2012

Danny and two teachers during a summer camp in Hangzhou, 2012

A river in Mentougou District, Beijing in 2018

Danny in a performance in Jingshi Experimental School in Mentougou District, Beijing, 2018

Danny in Sesame Street Language Center, Wuqing District, Tianjin

Students in Ping Ding Shan, Henan Province 2013

Danny and adult students in Ping Ding Shan, Henan Province, 2013

Danny at No 4 Middle school, Tianjin in 2014/ 2015

Danny and Yvonne at some hot springs in Yoashan Mountain, Ping Ding Shan, 2013

Danny giving a speech in TEDA District, Tianjin 2015

Danny and Yvonne at a nature park in Hebei Province in 2017

Teachers at a summer camp in Hangzhou in 2012

*Danny and another teacher named Michael in Jinan, the
capital city of Shandong Province, East China 2017*

Danny and Yvonne at a nature resort in 2017

*Danny and Michael in a nature park
in Jinan, Shandong Province*

Danny and Yvonne at a nature resort in Yangzhou, 2016

*Danny and Yvonne at a nature resort in Yangzhou
in 2016, Jiangsu Province*